Anot

Positive response to contemporary violence

Other books by Adam Curle

DEVELOPMENT, SOCIAL AND EDUCATIONAL
Educational Strategy for Developing Societies
Planning for Education in Pakistan
Educational Problems of Developing Societies
Education for Liberation

PEACE AND CONFLICT
Making Peace
True Justice
In the Middle
Tools for Transformation
Peace with Work to Do: The Academic Study of Peace
(with James O'Connell)

SOCIAL PSYCHOLOGY
Mystics and Militants

POETRY
Recognition of Reality

Another Way

Positive response to contemporary violence

ADAM CURLE

FOREWORD BY SCILLA ELWORTHY

JON CARPENTER
OXFORD

First published in 1995 by
Jon Carpenter Publishing
PO Box 129, Oxford OX1 4PH

The right of Adam Curle to be identified as author of this work has been
asserted in accordance with the Copyright, Designs and Patents Act 1988

ISBN 1 897766 22 X

Printed and bound by Biddles Ltd, Guildford and King's Lynn, England

Contents

Foreword

Reading the first half of this book made me wonder if Adam Curle might have become a pessimist in his later years — if perhaps the horrors he has witnessed, together with his shared sense of responsibility for what we are doing to our planet, might have convinced him that our time is running out too fast. I was quite wrong. This is a book about the toughness of love. It's about how, in the worst possible situations that we human beings can create for ourselves, love is the only response to fear that *works*.

There is no sentimentality. The enormity of humanity's distress is set out with unflinching clarity. While I thought I knew something of the extent to which violence has pervaded our lives, it required this kind of perspective to make me realise how fast our situation is becoming worse.

Women and men throughout the world, sitting talking round literally millions of kitchen tables, having discussions hunkered down in the dust, leaning over hundreds of thousands of desks, wounded or grieving in the aftermath of war, or simply lying anxious in their beds, are only too aware of this. The resulting emotions may be of anger or fear, energy or bitterness, or the courage born of awareness. But most of us do not know the way through. We do not know how to transform our capacity as human beings to hurt each other, into a potential to heal. Whether we are soldiers in uniform mandated to keep the peace, or diplomats involved in delicate negotiations, or advisers counselling the abused, or couples struggling to save a relationship — what we are short of is a set of principles to guide us through the maze of feelings that violence produces.

What we have here are the foundations of such a set of principles. Most are deeply rooted in our human development, or if you like, as old as the hills. What Adam Curle does is to call them out and make them live for us in the context of what is actually happening to people in these closing years of the twentieth century.

Most fundamentally, he shows us that change takes place not because of treaties, or inventions, or rationally devised solutions, but through the transformation of individuals. Our personal consciousness is ultimately what matters. If people involved in violence can change themselves and their reaction to violence, everything else changes. When it is a matter of a mere handful of people in Osijek, plunged in the terror of the Balkan conflict, challenging the daily routine violence of almost everyone around them, one wonders at first how their own personal change can make any difference. But it does. It does, for the simple reason that we are all interconnected. The recent development of chaos theory in all the sciences has formally recognised the interrelated nature of the universe. Chaos theory shows how tiny alterations in a system move through the system in apparently random ways to generate widespread changes. The classic example is the notion that the effect on the surrounding air molecules of the beating of a butterfly's wings on one part of the globe might trigger off a storm half way across the world.

By contrast, traditional physics used, and still uses, a model of how the world works which is a cause and effect model. It's a great model: it explains a lot, and has been the base of much technological innovation. But it has a tremendous limitation. The reasoning is, by its nature, linear and sequential. It all works fine until you come to complex systems. Try using the cause and effect model to predict what will happen in a family. Try using logic to sort out arguments!

The other model, well-known in eastern religions and philosophies, is interdependence. The Vietnamese Buddhist monk Thich Nhat Hahn said once, 'If I clap my hands, the effect is everywhere.' The new physics is thus adopting a model of the world which has been known to, and used by, much of humanity for a very long time. This book contains illustrations of how the principle of interconnectedness and interdependence works in people's lives today.

A second principle, which possibly follows from this, emerges again and again in the book. It is that it is not possible to solve a conflict using the same system of thought that generated it. We have to step outside that system of thought, as well as the language that defines the system to be as it is. This is why it doesn't work to send tired elderly western politicians to solve the problems of former Yugoslavia. Different systems of thought, and a different kind of communication, are necessary.

Real change comes about when people are enabled to use their thinking and their energy in a new way — using a different system of thought, different language, and having fresh visions of the future. Even in the case of entrenched domination power systems, it is important to remember that any different action, if it is sustained, brings about change.

A third principle, one which is as new to twentieth-century diplomacy as it is fundamental to ancient wisdom, is the psychological underpinning that is necessary for stable peace. A settlement can be *imposed* on warring factions, it can be *policed* or even *enforced*. But it will not itself bring about peace, for the simple reason that the underlying passions have not been addressed. The psychological damage caused by violence — the grief, hurt, anger, fear — does not simply dissolve. If unattended it festers into bitterness and demands revenge. Sooner or later it erupts in new violence. What is described here is the process of enabling both those of us who have done violence, and those to whom violence has been done, to transform our experience. Transforming it means ultimately to see the other not as an enemy but as another human being, in faults and virtues not so very unlike ourselves. This is slow, painstaking, unglamorous, *hard work*. It does not make the headlines. It is essential to peacemaking.

So is this book. It's an essential bit of kit in the backpack of a blue helmet, in the briefcase of a diplomat, on the desk of a marriage guidance counsellor, or in the bunker of a warlord. Even that can happen.

Scilla Elworthy
Oxford, June 1995

Acknowledgements

I did not realise, until I started to list them, to how many people I was in one way or another indebted for help in writing this book. I cannot list them all, but would like to mention a few who have been most directly involved in either the process of production or whose ideas and experience have been very important to me. Among the former are my wife Anne, who tirelessly read and re-read the manuscript for mistakes and solicisms, my daughter Deborah who used up her spare time retyping the whole thing onto a less archaic disk, and Jon Carpenter, whose critical skills and generous cooperation were most reassuring. I am also grateful to the Joseph Rowntree Charitable Trust for its generous contribution to my travelling costs and to the work on which the last part of this book is based.

Then there are those who contributed to the following pages. Firstly Scilla Elworthy who generously wrote the superb Foreword. Also Diana Francis, Roswitha Jarman and John McConnell who all wrote wisely about their training practice and principles for mediation and nonviolent action. And thanks too to Frank Cawson and Thomas Yeomans for their stimulating ideas.

I owe a deep debt to His Holiness the Dalai Lama for opening the doors of reality and to the late Lama Yeshe for his teachings on transformation; these have shaped many sections of the text, such as those concerned with the Three Poisons, change and how things happen.

I had the privilege of learning about many of the things discussed in these pages from Joseph Elder and the late Walter Martin through our companionship during four wars, two in Asia with Joe and two in Africa with Walter.

I am thankful to George Richert for the Esau Distinguished Visiting Professorship at Menno Simons College in the University of Winnipeg, which gave me the impetus to explore many of the topics discussed here.

I am most happy to express my gratitude to Margareta Ingelstam for what she has taught me about opposing violence through the construction of alliances for peace and security, and for her company during the episode described in the postscript to the final chapter.

Finally, of course, a great source of inspiration has been my friends in former Yugoslavia, principally the members of the Osijek Centre for Peace, Nonviolence and Human Rights, to whom this book is dedicated, but also Vesna Terselic who established the Anti-War Campaign in Zagreb and elsewhere, Manda and Ivan Prising, Vuk Stambolovic, and Bube Velat.

A.C.

Introduction

The horrible absurdities of the Cold War disastrously benumbed global good sense and political judgement. We believed the worst and in our fear did foolish things that made the worst more probable. Consequently, when Gorbachev's great initiative brought the Cold War to an end, when the Wall came down, when Eastern Europe liberated itself, we happily hailed what we were told was a New World Order. Until, that is, our euphoria was melted by the hot war in the Gulf and a healthy scepticism returned.

Since then, belief in almost every sort of order, new or old, has been eroded. It is true that there have been wonderful changes in South Africa and some promise of better things in Ireland and the Middle East. But the failure of political and sometimes military intervention by the United Nations or the European Union or the Organisation of African Unity or the United States or Russia, in Liberia, Somalia, Georgia, ex-Yugoslavia, and many other places, suggests a perilous unravelling of any concept of common security.

Another aspect of intervention by the powerful in the affairs of the poor and weak, is aid. Although ostensibly well intentioned, this has in general belied the hopes we had once had for it. Reasons for this failure are several and complex. They include the selfish interests of some donors who craftily mulct their clients of much more than they give them, policies based on ignorance and misunderstanding of local conditions, local inequalities and injustices, and the politico-economic stranglehold that the rich nations have over the poor ones. Although we shall be mainly concerned with the direct violence of armed conflict, discussion of economic issues is far from irrelevant: poverty and inequality are major elements in the culture of anomie and violence. So, paradoxically, is the material prosperity of the market if, as so often, it is achieved at the expense of close human relations and family cohesion.

Our loss of faith in a stable and controllable world order is encouraged by increasing awareness of the myriad armed struggles throughout the planet. Some are full blown wars involving large armies and causing thousands of casualties (now nearly always over eighty per cent civilian — if you want to stay alive, join the army). But an almost countless number of smaller groups are clawing each other to pieces, some incessantly and over long periods, some with sporadic desperation.

In the past, even only thirty years ago when I was first involved in international peacemaking, wars were more comprehensible. They were fought for territory, to retain or to liberate colonies, to over-throw tyrants, or as proxy wars of the Cold War powers. Many of these were highly intractable (one proxy war — in Angola — seems at last to be ending, though the patrons have long since withdrawn), but not completely unamenable to well-tried methods of peace-making intervention. And the UN writ still ran. The 1965 war between Pakistan and India was brought to an end after three weeks at the order of the Security Council. (Some cynics say it is because both sides ran out of ammunition, but it is hardly likely that this happened to each simultaneously).

Not so today. The approaches of the UN and other bodies are spurned, deflected or ignored. We respond with lack of resolve, with confusion and, at times, with inappropriate violence (as did the US in Somalia) that only makes things worse. There are many reasons for this, but one is certainly that we do not *understand* the motives for these conflicts. The explanation could be that there may be nothing to understand, that many of them are in fact entirely pointless. People throughout the globe are killing and torturing each other for no observable political, ideological or territorial purpose, nothing beyond the crazed ambition of some autistic warlord.

But there is, of course, an inner purpose. These people are, for reasons we shall discuss, full of fear and anger, desperation and despair. They no longer belong to or believe in anyone or anything, and violence is their only anodyne for alienation.

However, we all know from our own experience, wheresoever we may live, that pointless violence is not confined to shooting wars in distant places. The armed mobs of Liberia or Afghanistan heedlessly lay waste their own country; the equally alienated youth of London, Manchester, Los Angeles, Rio, Lagos or New York smash their own habitats (as well as raping old women and battering them to death), destroying the very amenities they may need tomorrow, or even today — the hospitals, the public telephones, the parks, the public toilets. The anguished boredom of anomie needs no passport.

Why should this be? The Cold War must take some of the blame. Everyone alive today, except the very young, has spent the greater part of his or her life under the mushroom shroud which, by threatening universal death, stole the point of living. But it also bred a fearsomely competitive materialism: while you live, live it up; never mind the rosebuds (or indeed the other bugger), but gather whatever the ads say will make you happy.

And these psychological factors were, I suspect, exacerbated by the increasingly rapid rate of change during the second half of the century. The jet engine, the silicon chip, the antibiotic and the television have transformed both social structures and aspirations far beyond the scope of our capacity to adjust creatively to them, as we more easily could during the gradual evolution of earlier ages.

Now things are happening to us all, not just to the young, which we don't know how to cope with. I think particularly of the widening gap globally between rich and poor countries, and — also globally — the growing proportion of the population that *is* poor. Anger and helplessness are an explosive and irrational compound.

The world is full of do-gooders who aren't sure what is good or how to do it. The moral centre seems to be falling apart; our struggles to reconstruct it through such means as deconstruction are in vain. In general we are simply trying to solve our problems by using the disproved concepts and methods that created them, the stale diplomacy, the shallow understanding of human nature, the futile belief in brute force.

The bloody picture I have been painting began to become horridly clear in 1991 when the Serbs invaded Croatia, razed Vukovar and ruthlessly attacked Osijek.

The other side of the coin

Here, however, I must modify the image of encroaching and intensifying violence I have been trying to delineate. There is another side to the chaotic change that has followed on the cataclysm of two World Wars. Alongside the cruelty, extremism and alienation there is a growth of understanding and compassion. There is a return to what humanity has always known, but has tended to forget in the glittering but superficial galaxies of material advancement and social change: that love and friendship are more important for our happiness than wealth, which indeed often threatens it. This oblivion has had two destructive effects.

The first is that many have become agnostics. We have discarded respect or belief in what could not be weighed, measured or described by objective means. Morality, soul, compassion retained a type of sentimental value, but became insignificant as bases for action.

Or, secondly, some have become passionate devotees of one

dogma or another (credos which others of us would regard as being just as irrational as the idea of a soul) for which they would be prepared to kill or be killed, or — depending on the social and religious context — to ruin or neglect.

Oddly enough these two antithetical groups equally promote brutal violence. Both are oblivious of the most fundamental and universal facts of human nature: that it is intrinsically sound and unflawed, albeit on the surface, and indeed often deeply, confused and deluded by our accumulation of unassuaged pains and misconceptions. (This ignorance is discussed at some length later.)

Because of this, we are largely unaware of the wonderful potentials of our nature for wisdom, compassion and courage. These are our heritage. We don't obtain them through any effort of will or prayer. We cannot say that they are ours personally, because they are ubiquitous.

You may wonder how I can state this as a fact and not as a belief — that is to say, something I hold to be true because it has been told to me by some authority I trust. No, I have found in my own life that this is so; that if I act on the assumption that people, including you and me, have these capacities, those persons will then manifest them. They will most probably not manifest them completely, but more so than before. And if they continue to have faith in their capacities, these will increasingly pierce the gloom of fear and misconception.

And this, it seems to me, is happening with more and more people, mostly young, throughout the world. They are still very much the minority. But my generation of youth had no idea whatsoever of such possibilities. Today they are sought by many paths. Some follow the traditional churches; some through Eastern religion, particularly Buddhism; some again through various psychological systems, through many forms of services to others, through humanistic atheism, and naturally through the infinitely various courses of their regular lives.

But whatever they hold to be the most practicable system of ideas, whichever seems most clearly to reflect more universal truths, they have a vision of unity. They have a sense of the oneness of humanity if not of all life. Most importantly, they have a sense of the basic goodness of life and, therefore, respect for all others. To this is joined both the desire and the ability to help them in their needs and to awaken in them the same awareness.

It is in these women and men that we must, I am sure, place our hopes for a diminution of the violence, the violence against both humanity and nature, that threatens us all.

The basis of this book

Until the beginning of the Balkan wars, my efforts at peacemaking had been basically political, or rather executed through a political process. I had always recognised that in practice they followed psychological principles, but the ultimate objective was a peace agreement that could be defined in political terms.

Now I began to see things differently. There had to be settlement, of course, which would require the assent of those in a position to take important decisions. But now I saw clearly that there must be more widespread changes of heart; that even if the leaders agreed (probably out of expediency rather than a conviction of the *rightness* of peace), no real peace would ensue. I was further convinced by meeting people who were acting out the vision of unity and the principle of a human nature that is basically good. I am deeply grateful to my friends in former Yugoslavia for the opportunity to work with and learn from them and so, at this late stage in my life, to find a different way to approach the issues of violence and war.

I came to realise that it was time for me to learn a new peace instrument on which I could play a different sort of music; one better suited to our cruel times. The pages which follow lead to an account of this new tune, this new instrument.

Part I explores and tried to define the nature of violence. Is it an inevitable consequence of our genetic constitution; or does it arise from a faulty understanding of our nature? What are its social roots? Has it changed recently and if so, has this been brought about the by rapidity of social change? It concludes with a tentative diagnosis and epidemiology.

Part II considers the potentiality and the limitations of human beings as peacemakers; the scope of mediation in both violent and nonviolent situations; and the danger that intervention in peacemaking or aid giving may only end up as dangerous interference. It ends with an examination of some more recent, and promising, approaches.

Part III tries to describe the new instrument; the nature and the growth of a Peace Centre in Osijek, Croatia which may provide one model for an antidote to the lethal prevalence of alienation, and for the relations of the outsider, individual or international agency, with groups snared in conflict.

Part I
Violence

Introduction to Part I

This first part of this book was the most difficult and confusing to
write; I hope it will not equally affect the reader. The subject, and
indeed that of virtually the whole book, is violence. But the context
is vast and the facets countless, very hard to weave into a coherent
whole. I hope the few lines which follow will be helpful.

I begin with an attempt to define the word, and progress to what
the word portends: the horror, the dirtiness, the pain. We look briefly,
and without enthusiasm, at the idea that violence is innate (and so
presumably can be 'excused'). We then consider in greater detail the
Buddhist psycho-philosophical concept of the Three Poisons, as the
Tibetans call it. Among many approaches to the problems of violence
with which, being originally a psychologist, I have attempted to work,
I find this the most convincing conceptually and in practice.

Without the theological inescapability of the dogma of original
sin, it shows how very difficult it is for us to avoid completely the
negative emotions — the acquisitive urges, jealousy, vanity, anger,
dislike, prejudice. These lead easily to violence of feelings or of
action. Moreover, even if they do not much affect us personally, their
prevalence lends them a certain tolerance or acceptance in many
cultures in which they form the staple subject matter of literature and
the more sensational media. The crucial poison is ignorance; ignorance of the potential of our nature. However, ignorance can be
overcome, and with it the proclivity for violence.

There follow several chapters and parts of chapters dealing with
the context of violence. These concern, for example, the effects of
decolonisation in Africa, the development of the nation state (in
which a considerable part was played by the need felt by monarchs
to build up and control their armed services), the growth of a global
'culture of militarism', the violence of the cities. The chapter on The
Speed of Change identifies this with the growth of alienation; this
appears to be the condition most conducive to violence.

Part I ends with a discussion of this diagnosis. This leads on to the
remaining two parts, which have already been mentioned in the
general Introduction, and the Conclusion.

Finally, we have to remember that we are all creatures of the jungle,
some the victims and some the predators, often changing roles,
sometimes playing both simultaneously — little boys, perhaps victims
of a bully, avenging our distress on a yet smaller child. We must learn
to view the scene objectively and with engaged compassion; only thus
can we diminish the miseries, terrors and dreadful compulsions to hurt
that could otherwise be passed on to further generations.

Violence: the mental roots

The grim disappointments of the post-Cold War world made it impossible for us to rest on our few, withered laurels. We now face a world smouldering, even when it is not blazing, with civil wars, many of them genocidal. The enemy is violence.

A military dictum urges, 'Known Your Enemy'. What *is* violence? What does the word actually mean?

Definition of violence

The derivation of the words 'violent' and 'violence' implies (at least in English and languages such as French where it has the same Latin derivation) the excessive or illegal use of force. They suggest the violation or the rape of a person; dirtiness and brutality; action which smears its object; a horrible or wilful intrusion into a person's life or body. Torture. Something antihuman.

Violence is something which does harm to people; harm in the sense of words, deeds, or situations which damage the ability to develop fully the human potential for feeling, creation and happy maturity.

A very angry and tormented person I once knew would justify her rages by quoting Jesus: 'The violent take heaven by force'. I hope she succeeded in this, but she certainly caused great pain to others in the process. The following pages try to show that violence, as I shall describe it, can never be justified.

Violence may be contrasted with simple force or pressure which may be used to constrain or control, but does not damage.

It may also be compared with conflict. This is a word often used ambiguously to mean either something as violent as war, or as innocuous and even creative as a difference of opinion.

I use 'conflict' to mean conflicts of interest which, although they may degenerate, need be no more harmful than a friendly disagreement about where to spend the family holiday.

Finally, violence may also be thought of as the opposite of peace; as the ultimate form of unpeace, a combination of cruelty and disorder. Peace is not easy to define, but I should try to do it so that the identification of violence may be sharpened.

Peace

Peace, in truth, is a difficult word, being both emotive and abstract. To some, it is a remote and impractical state of beatitude, wonderful but probably unattainable; to others it suggests a weak or even traitorous caving in to the enemy (this interpretation of the word brought much unpopularity to peace groups at the height of the Cold War, and of course during the white feather campaign of World War I); but perhaps to most it just means a state of no-war, even including such situations as when rulers (or colonial powers) held down resentful and unhappy subjects, preventing violence by the threat and demonstration of force. And the words in other languages which are translated in English as peace have implications in their own tongues as varied as law and order, submission to the will of God, harmony, and prosperity. I remember also the cynical Roman quoted by Tacitus: 'They make a desert and they call it peace', a good slogan for opponents of the Vietnam war.

Searching for a more accurate way of defining peace, I found it more appropriate to think in terms of peaceful and unpeaceful relationships.

Putting it shortly, peaceful relationships would be ones in which the various parties did each other more good than harm; whereas unpeaceful ones would be those doing more harm than good. The advantage of this terminology was that it would cover any exigency of human relationships: interpersonal (even intrapersonal), familial, communal, international, and so on.

Between a man and a woman, for example, a peaceful relationship, despite perhaps occasional tiffs, would in general provide for mutual support, comfort, and a pleasurable life; in an unpeaceful relationship, one or both of the couple would make the other feel anxious, guilty, inadequate, frustrated, angry, etc., and their life would be more unhappy than happy.

A peaceful relationship between larger groups, such as states, would be characterised by close and relaxed political and economic ties, ensuring that if any differences arose they would be quickly and amicably resolved. An unpeaceful relationship would be the opposite; serious differences might lead to breach of diplomatic relations, dangerous confrontations and even in the last resort to war. Situations of oppression, which tyrants have often whitewashed as 'peaceful', would be characterised as unpeaceful relations between the oppressors, who profited from the cheap labour of those they oppressed, while the latter suffered the material disadvantages, the humiliation and the degradation that their fellows in South Africa suffered under apartheid.

What characterises unpeaceful, as opposed to peaceful, relations is, of course, their violence towards human beings. It may be the direct violence of person to person; or the violence of a system that legislates unjustly towards various categories of people — for example, gypsies in parts of Europe; or an economic structure which, without actual malevolence but certainly uncaring, ensures the prosperity of the rich at the expense of the poor.

Unpeaceful relations, modern style

It is perhaps misleading to claim that there is a modern form of violence; violence has been around a long time, and been manifested in many horrid shapes. I believe, however, that a certain sort of violence is considerably more prevalent than even a few decades ago. It could be characterised as *pointless*.

A young man needing money to feed a drug addiction or to buy a pair of trainers, mugs an old woman and steals her slender purse. But having done so, he kicks and punches her until she is unrecognisable. Why? He had got what he wanted except, we must suppose, satisfaction for some pathological inner need. (I speak of a young man, not because I am a complaining old one, but because the actions of the young are a thermometer by which to judge the health of the society as a whole; their parents and grandparents have their own vices which may be less obvious only because they are so common).

Other persons, and not necessarily young ones, do not so much hurt others, but themselves. Unlike animals, to which they are sometimes compared, they soil and spoil their own environmental habitat, trashing the bus shelters, telephone booths, the public toilets they many need to use tomorrow. They pollute the streets and their housing estate or apartment block with the abundant detritus of modern life — quick food wrappings, empty lager and soft drink cans, condoms, and broken glass from bottles and shattered windows. They smash the lights of the walkways, creating a dark, miserable and dangerous milieu in which they and their families live, trapped by poverty and the inertia of despair.

This destructive degradation of homes and lives serves only to dig deeper the pit of wretchedness and alienation. It is utterly without real purpose.

Nor are most of the hundred or so armed struggles throughout the world (over thirty are considered as wars, having over 1000 fatal casualties per year). The insane cruelties of Bosnia, the horrifying massacres of Rwanda and Burundi, the clan warfare of Somalia, the aimless butchery of Cambodia, the dazed boy soldiers of Mozambique or Liberia, the futile continuation of war in Afghanistan long after the defeat of the Russian army; all this and so much more, surely suggests something new, if only in scale. What I have myself seen suggests that this endless, pointless brutality is carried out by those for whom violence is the only drug for anomic despair in a world they can no longer understand or accept — and so destroy.

It is, of course, true that many of these conflicts began in desperate and understandable reactions to intolerable oppression, the pressures of famine and general scarcity of resources, or rivalries over the possession of land (such as are frequent in the former USSR, where Stalin's exiles returned to find their fields in alien hands). Others developed from ideological clashes, religious fanaticism, North/South rivalry and polarisation, the carry-over of Cold War postures, fears or hopes fuelled by increasing global militarism, and local arms races. Some were fomented by agents of powerful states, posing as diplomats. Many approached the conflict in a spirit of idealism, which some may still retain. On the whole, however, although the impetus of the violence survives, its original objectives have been eroded. The mindless slaughter and the cruelty seem to have developed their own momentum.

Even within my own local experience, things have changed. The streets of London are no longer safe — my daughter who lives there has been attacked three times. Homes are locked up carefully which never used to be. Cars parked on the roads, if not stolen, are casually mutilated. People slink past each other in the street, head averted lest eye contact should provoke assault. Children now carry arms, and even use them on each other as well as on adults; they become drug-addicted; they are forced to sleep in the streets by a nation grown callous (certainly a form of violence).

We can, I suppose, at least be thankful that they are not murdered here as they are in Brazil by semi-official death squads. But any society in which any of these things regularly happen without raising an enormous outcry is surely brutally sick.

Wars, of course, have always provoked occasional atrocities, but in relatively recent European history at any rate, civilians were not involved; there was no military genocide. Wars were waged for understandable motives to regain territory, to eject a colonial power, to overthrow a tyrant, to separate from a distasteful majority rule. Three of the wars in which I was involved as a would-be mediator earlier in my career were of this sort: Pakistan striving to liberate predominantly Muslim Kashmir from Hindu India; Zimbabwe struggling with the colonial-type government of white Rhodesia; Biafra wanting independence from the rest of Nigeria, stigmatised as genocidal (though of course the issue was more complicated and less exculpatory than this might suggest).

Now, however, 'reasonable' motives are all too often superseded by the furies of fanaticism or, even worse, the violence of men become automata whose only reflex is to press the trigger. This is why violence on whatever scale and in whatever setting is so difficult to deal with, either to forestall or to bring to a sensible conclusion. The failures of governments and police concerned with today's anarchic violence and crime should not be attributed entirely to blundering stupidity. They are facing something for which experience and training had not prepared them; the old remedies are long past their sell-by date, or the problems are on a scale beyond their competence to affect. Out of their depth, the authorities are trying to cope with crime by escalating penalties, but they merely fill the prisons and create a new and larger generation of incorrigible (in the true sense of uncorrectable) young people, their gaol experience having merely confirms their contempt for society.

The roots of violence: congenital aggression

Friends have often told me (and I suspect that many think it if they haven't actually said so) that I am wasting my life trying to work for peace. Their argument is that human beings are violent by nature and that there is nothing anyone can do about it. I answer that there is a great deal we can do about it; surely they know examples of really nasty quarrels, large scale or small, that someone has wisely defused. Moreover, I add that whether or not we have an innate aggressive or violent streak is a less important issue than whether or not we can guide this force (whatever its source) into constructive effort.

The argument for congenital aggression is often bolstered by the observation by ethologists of animal behaviour. It is well known that animals (including birds and some fish) will fight others to guard their mates or offspring, to secure a mate or to protect their territory. However, in these struggles they very seldom kill any of their own kind (though an alien may be slain); and so far as I know ants are the only creatures besides ourselves who war against each other. In intra-species fights for supremacy in herd, etc., the loser will offer his jugular to the victor's coup de grace but the winner will ignore it and just stalk on.

We probably share with most of the animal kingdom a utilitarian impulse of potentially violent aggression when our vital interests, or those of our group (family or nation) are imperilled. But this can hardly be employed as an explanation or excuse for the barbarity of our violence.

To be sure, not all members of the same animal species behave pleasantly to each other. My wife and I would watch from our balcony at the University of Delhi guest house a tribe of monkeys which invaded the lawn every evening. The older males did not behave nicely to the younger ones, whom they would cuff if they came too near. There were occasional fights, but they were never very serious. We never saw injuries inflicted and certainly nothing like a deadly quarrel, or a war with a neighbouring group.

But unlike the animals, we humans slaughter each other and in huge numbers. We inflict pain and suffering in many loathsome and destructive ways as though they were natural, proper and even laudable. We glorify war, for example. Armed men, parades of weapons, gaudy uniforms, martial music tend to be central to our national celebrations.

The proverbial visitor from Mars might characterise human culture (as opposed to that of other terrestrial creatures) as being one in which mutual slaughter was a dominant feature.

Naturally, there is obviously very much more to human behaviour than violence. We love one another; we build complex social structures for living together and caring for each other; we are amazingly intelligent; we create beautiful things; we have great and largely untapped potentials.

But do not these gifts make it even harder to account for the prevalence of human violence? We might have thought that our sensitivity would have made us abhor it, and that if circumstances seem to force it on us, our abilities would have enabled us to find peaceful alternatives. (And of course this happens often, and we shall discuss these alternatives at length; but wars happen too).

It is unfortunately obvious that we are very prone to violence. This cannot be fully explained as an expression of the aggressive programming we share with animals. There must, then, be something more, some idiosyncratic qualities of *human* nature.

Two of these may be explained by what I call the **Leopard Parable** and the **Toy Gun Illusion**.

The Leopard Parable derives, paradoxically, from those very capacities which might be thought to preclude violence — our imagination, a brain that enables us to think ahead, and the very sensitivity just mentioned. These are qualities less well developed in, say, monkeys. If one of them is frightened by a marauding leopard, it shows every symptom of terror, gibbering and rushing to the highest branch of its tree. But as soon as the danger is past it calmly continues feeding.

A human in such circumstances might move to another part of the forest, install a leopard alarm, buy a gun. He might be haunted by fear of the leopard, develop ulcers, lose his appetite. He might decide that he could never enjoy life while the leopard lived, and so would have to kill it. He would declare war against the leopard and devote his energies to training and planning for it. His sons would also be enlisted. It would be instilled into them that it was their family duty to take part in the war against the leopard. One day, one of them would be killed by the leopard, and the sorrowing father would say; 'How right we were to fight this wicked creature; our efforts to destroy it must be redoubled and our weapons improved'. The mutual hostility and hatred would go on for generations, each disaster providing fresh justification for their continuation.

The Toy Gun Illusion could be called the 'Happiness' or the 'If Only' Illusion. 'If only I won the lottery, if only I had a decent home... I would be forever happy.'

I call this the Toy Gun Illusion because when I was five, I longed for a particular toy gun and believed that 'if only' I possessed it I would never want anything else; I would always be happy. However, my mother who had lost three brothers in World War I was an ardent pacifist, hating all weapons or any imitations of them. But at length I wore her down.

The gun was mine and I was deliriously happy.

A couple of days later, however, some now forgotten occurrence upset me. I wept bitterly. But even as I cried, I thought to myself, 'No, I was wrong. The gun can't make me permanently happy; happiness comes from inside, and external objects or happenings cannot affect our inner state except for a short time'. I don't know how I put this to myself, not in these words certainly. But I remember vividly the essence of my thoughts and can recall the physical setting of thinking them.

On countless subsequent occasions I have thought how pleasant it would be to have, meet, see, hear, know, smell, someone/thing or other. My yearning, however, has almost always been tempered by the knowledge that the satisfaction I yearned for would not last.

And I came to understand something else as well. Not only would the satisfaction not endure, but the person, thing or situation would not last either. The person we wished to be with would die, move away, fail to reciprocate our love, lose the qualities which had endeared her/him to us. And comparable changes would affect everything, human or otherwise, that we longed for. The toy gun would break, be mislaid, or just lose its appeal! It is symptomatic that although I remember being given it so clearly, I have no recollection whatsoever of what happened to it.

So, the Toy Gun Illusion, the illusion of 'if only', is generally made up of two illusions. One is that happiness is conferred by something outside ourselves. The other is that happiness is permanent. We would no doubt deny this at an intellectual level; we know that the one we love will die. But we don't really believe it. The day we first realise that we love each other, we feel it will last forever. This is why we are so happy. However, although we constantly try to freeze the preconditions for happiness (as we perceive them and it) like a mammoth in the tundra, everything, always, is in a state of change. Everything outside us changes, and everything inside too. Nothing is ever the same as it was ten years, ten minutes or ten seconds ago. It is the same for stones as for human beings. At whatever level, cellular, molecular, atomic, or emotional, there is change.

And although we yearn for stability and permanence, and foster the illusion of possessing these qualities in our lives (except, of course, when things are going badly!), it is good that we don't have them. I am reminded of the father who bewailed the passage of his charming little daughter into gawky adolescence; 'Surely', the mother said, 'you don't want her to remain eleven all her life?'

How is it then that these two illusions, of the external causation of the inner state of happiness and of permanence (especially permanent happiness), cause violence?

They suggest to us that we can achieve happiness, indeed permanent happiness, by manipulating events and environments rather than changing ourselves. The stronger this belief, the greater the lengths to which we will go in order to sustain it. In the final resort we may angrily damage or destroy whatever we feel obstructs our quest for happiness. Moreover, this illusion enables us conveniently to conceal (from ourselves as well as others) unpleasant impulses of greed and hatred, using such grandiose slogans as resisting aggression or fighting for freedom and justice. The search for satisfaction or revenge becomes morally respectable; exploitation of others or the environment is seen to be entrepreneurially acceptable.

Another way of describing this cluster of illusions is ignorance.

The roots of violence: the Three Poisons

Ignorance is the first of the Three Poisons of the mind, according to Tibetan psycho-philosophers. It is not ignorance of facts or ideas, of illiteracy or innumeracy, not of the rules of grammar, or international affairs, or psychoanalysis, or modern art. It is ignorance of our nature. This ignorance is harmful because it leads to a false perception of reality, which in turn leads to behaviour causing suffering to ourselves and others. The essence of our ignorance is the belief that we, and everyone else, are all separate and self-existent beings (and thus we believe, as we have seen, that we are able to organise the external to promote and sustain what is internal — our happiness). We fail to see ourselves as being the sum product of every influence that has played upon us since and even before our birth — genetic and psychological, social and academic, cultural and physical, familial and communal, spiritual and material. Since these influences cannot be static and are constantly being altered or added to, the 'I', the entity on which they impinge, is forever changing. There is no permanent I or you. This we find hard to accept.

We don't realise that tomorrow we shall be slightly different because our circumstances are slightly different; the weather has changed, the news in the papers is different, we sit next to different people on bus or train, we are twenty-four hours older, new things have happened in the world. We are probably not aware of all this, but the totality of our environment, its interacting outer and inner elements, will be other than they were today. We have this illusion of an unchanging and independent self, which distinguishes us and isolates us from all the other unchanging and independent selves by whom we are surrounded.

(I am in no sense suggesting that we are puppets. We are not beings that lack will or individuality because we are affected by a vast number of influences. On the contrary, we are highly individual because all these influences impinge differently on us, evoking different responses simply because we *are* different).

What we have in common is mind, the capacity that underlies the confusion and turbulence of our conscious thinking process. The Tibetans refer to this as Mind. Jung calls it the Self and relates it to the collective unconscious. The mediaeval mystics called it the Ground of our Being and thought of it as God, but we can each choose our psychological or theological terms.

The idea of Mind can be transferred to the wider reality of, for example, a tree or a plant. No less than ourselves, these are subject to many influences: the climate and its variations, the soil, the air (and currently its pollutants), its heredity. Any gardener knows that these combine with different effects, so that flowers or vegetables planted in slightly different places and at slightly different times will develop differently. But each will develop in accordance with an inner scheme, a shared programme, a shared and universal capacity. But when we look at another person, or a lettuce, or an ant, we tend to see a separate being, someone/thing existing on its own. Still more so, we see ourselves and that lettuce or ant as living quite independently of each other. But of course we are not, as every ecologist knows. *We are all part of the body of influences that form each other.* We interact, we inter-are.

To the extent that we realise this, not in the sense of accepting it as an abstract intellectual proposition, but of letting it become *real* within ourselves, of *knowing* it, we must see things differently. We see them as they truly are, not through the lens of ignorance as independent objects, but as forming part of a unitary environment of which we are also a part.

How, in the light of this realisation, can we act violently towards any form of life, or indeed to anything inanimate that affects life? To hurt another being is to hurt ourselves; war becomes an unthinkable option.

The implications of this realisation are of course delicate and complex. They involve matters of personal choice regarding, for example, diet and living style. But they also expand into a vast range of public issues to do with violence towards the environment with which we, as individuals, are also concerned. I must, however, leave these for others, like Ken Jones (see Bibliography), who are better qualified to deal with them, and myself concentrate on the violence of human beings towards each other.

However, to the extent that we remain ignorant of our true nature, we suffer. Our ignorance cuts us off from the reality of our existence. Things seem vaguely unsatisfactory; in the midst of our friends, we may feel lonely; there is often an obscure sense of things not being quite right. We are somehow off balance, plagued by guilt for we know not what. We sense that we are cut off from something precious, but unknown.

The second poison is the **Yearning, Longing, Wanting, Lusting Greed** that is generated by this sense of insufficiency and loss. We are obsessed by the need to compensate for our loneliness and inadequacy, somehow to show to ourselves, even more than to others, that we are worthwhile beings. We make up for the feeling of lack by getting, by acquisition. We yearn greedily for whatever it may be that will bring us happiness and fulfilment, that will assuage our guilt by demonstrating to our inner judge that we can't be quite as bad as we sometimes feel we are.

One effect of ignorance is to make us feel we have no power over our lives. And a common response is to yearn for the things that demonstrate power: wealth and position. By lording it over others we unconsciously hope to prove (to ourselves) that we are not really impotent.

This, of course, is relative. We don't have to be prime minister or a billionaire. It may well suffice to be able to dominate spouse or partner, children or colleagues. It may satisfy us to have enough to cut a dash with the neighbours — not merely to keep up with the Jones's but preferably to overtake them in the modish decor of our home or the exclusive make of our car.

Some of us may not strive for power, wealth, high office, or possessions. We may hope to be recognised for qualities of mind or character, for our knowledge of the French impressionists or the contemporary novel, for our wit or for our profundity, our athletic ability or our appearance. There is an endless variety of skills, qualities and experiences by means of which we try to mend the ravages of inner doubt and guilt. Some we may hug to ourselves, others we project onto others in the hope that their envy, esteem or fear will make up for our hidden sense of unworthiness.

Out of all these things we build up an ego, an identity, an image of a self we can feel proud of; one we half-believe we possess. It is our defence against insecurity, despair and our feelings of futility. But it is very fragile. The things on which it is built are impermanent: often the very methods we use to achieve power will alienate those we most wish to impress, thus reawakening our nightmare of impotence. Or the Jones's will in some way overtake us. Or our looks will fade, our shares lose their value, our writings or paintings be panned by the critics.

The essence of this second poison is desiring. This, obviously, is part of the Toy Gun Illusion. We want a Thing because of the effect we hope it will have on the mind, even if only one's own mind. But it can become obsessively strong — craving and lusting rather than simply wanting. But once we have entered this world of competitive materialism we are inevitably at risk.

The third poison follows inexorably from the eventual failures and disappointments of the second. It is characterised by **Jealousy and Hatred**. We are jealous of those who have run faster in the rat race. We hate those who have thwarted us in achieving what we long to do. We are full of anger and frustration because things haven't worked out properly.

For a moment we reluctantly and resentfully face our declining powers, but then rapidly summon up fresh fantasies to deny them.

Maybe you are sufficiently enlightened to avoid these negative, basically hostile feelings. But most of us, from time to time, have a sense

that things are slightly out of kilter, that something's missing. We turn
on the TV or have a drink and forget about it, or talk to our friends, or
help someone who is in difficulty. But the vague feeling that some
unidentified thing is mysteriously not quite right still returns occasionally to haunt us. It may be there are a number of things we don't
like very much, or people we don't get on with, or work we dislike;
some small facet of imperfection, nothing very important, but a stark
contrast to the occasional experience we may have had of true bliss.
And true bliss is a taste of reality, which shows up everything else.

In short, the essence of the third poison is negative feelings,
ranging from slight distaste to angry loathing. These circle round to
heighten ignorance by further clouding our perceptions of truth. In
Tibetan iconography they are depicted as a swine, a snake and a
cockerel endlessness circling as they bite each other's tails.

The Three Poisons provide the basis of selfishness, alienation
from others, acquisitive greed, competitiveness, and dislike, from
which most violence grows. Because of their virtual universality they
have almost been elevated to the status of theological dogma as a
form of original sin. However, the Three Poisons cycle is a formula-
tion of Buddhism, of which the central precept is that the cause of
suffering, including of course the states of mind that lead to violence,
can be identified and nullified, not by God, but by our own efforts.

It should be added, moreover, that the character of the society will
determine the type and intensity of the violence and other ills it gener-
ates. In neolithic Europe, for example, with its predominantly female
deities and egalitarian society, the level of large-scale violence would
appear to have been low, compared with today's successive slaughters.

Pain

To conclude this section on the mental roots of violence, I must refer
to pain. It is, of course, subsumed in the whole cycle of the Three
Poisons. It is because life is not as we would wish it to be that we
suffer and are driven into actions and attitudes which prolong or
preserve that suffering. We may not think of it as such, since the
word tends for us to have rather extreme implications of anguish. But
the *dukkha* — the Sanskrit word in Buddhist writings which is translated as suffering — refers in general to a nagging under layer of
worry or dissatisfaction in our minds which from time to time bursts
through in anger, depression or despair — and occasionally, of
course, in violence.

But there are also extreme forms of suffering which are very hard
to withstand and which lead to deeply embedded and lasting pain.

These include loneliness, loss and rejection, particularly in childhood and within the family, exposure to great violence as in war, traumatic social conditions such as famine, eviction from home, imprisonment, or destitution.

Such experiences, unless exorcised or excised by the priestly confessional or on the therapeutic couch, are apt to leave an unhealed psychic wound. This may break out in a variety of forms: exaggerated yearning, fears, or prejudices; psychological or related physical illness; aberrant or antisocial behaviour; or violence towards others or against the self. Many of these projections of pain might currently be defined as post-traumatic stress.

A great danger for the world is that the last few decades have seen such a number of wars, such social upheaval, so many brutal state regimes, so many millions of people displaced from their homes. The quantity of people who have suffered extreme pain is immeasurably huge. Sadly, those whose reactions to it are violent will merely heighten and expand the realm of suffering and extend it into the next generation — this is the meaning of the Biblical saying that the sins (in this case the impact of pain) of fathers will be visited upon their children and indeed future generations.

This most terrible of vicious circles constitutes a grave and pitiful danger to humanity.

Violence: some social and historical contexts

To counteract the violence of today it is helpful to understand something of its roots. In this chapter I want to suggest that the expressions of violence as we know them today, in the 1990s, may have been different in the past and that the contemporary precipitating factors have evolved over the centuries. We, the human beings who act violently or who try to prevent violence, are no doubt fundamentally the same as our ancestors; the relevance of philosophical and religious beliefs more than two thousand years old suggest that this is so. We have, however, created a world in which the pressures on perhaps the majority of us are very different. The next few pages constitute an effort to recognise the changes and to identify the pressures.

A historical perspective

People sometimes speak as though we had emerged, although with unfortunate lapses, from a state of barbarity to which primitive humanity was prone, into 'modern society' which is orderly and urbane. It seems to be assumed that violence is something primitive. 'They behaved like savages', we are told of some particularly destructive act. 'Civilised people should have known better than that'. Indeed they should, but in fact the tribal peoples, peasants, nomads, herdsmen and others whom my uncles used to refer to as savages or primitives were much less prone to destructive behaviour than are we.

We learn how peaceable they were from many sources. From records of early travellers, going back as far as Herodotus, from great collections of anthropological data such as James Frazer's *The Golden Bough,* and from much more recent or even contemporary ethnologists and explorers of surviving stone age cultures, we can see how the practice of war developed with the growth of our social complexity. In fact the Tasaday, a minute tribe discovered a few decades ago in the Philippines, have no words whatsoever for quarrel, fight, war, or any sort of violence; and this is not unique. Virtually no type of communal violence seems, in fact, to have predated the shift from hunting and gathering to settled agriculture when competition for water and other resources became influential. In fact a study by Broch and Galtung (*Journal of Peace Research*, Vol 11, No 1, 1966) shows that out of 625 preliterate societies only a third engaged in anything comparable to warfare.

There is now also a considerable weight of evidence that neolithic Europe was not only extremely peaceful, but by modern democratic ideals, nonhierarchical. It was only destroyed by the incursions of militaristic (and hence hierarchical) barbarian hordes from further east. The subtle and delightful civilisation of Crete was the last to fall to these invaders, whose aggressive and stratified power-based culture has become almost global.

In the simplest societies, lethal fighting was unknown. If two groups, clans or tribes quarrelled they might confront each other dressed in impressive garb, including perhaps feathers, paints, and horned head gear. There would be much stamping, shouting of insults, and waving and then hurling of spears. But the groups would be carefully drawn up beyond the range of each others' flying weapons. Or they would shoot arrows, but the feathers (unlike the feathers on those they used for hunting), would be so affixed that accurate aiming was impossible. These pseudo-bellicose procedures would mollify any sense of insult or affront.

As the groups became more complex, these conflicts would become more dangerous. The arrows flew straighter, the spears reached their targets, but the engagement was abruptly called off if anyone was killed or, in some cases, wounded. Honour was satisfied.

In fact, there was often a ceremonial quality about war until very recently. In the time of the Duke of Marlborough (1650–1722), the opposing armies would line up facing each other; their generals would ride out to greet each other; and only when they had returned to their own lines would the bugle call for the affray to start. The Battle of Waterloo, almost a hundred years after Marlborough's death, although a historically crucial conflict, was also almost a social event. The wives and mistresses of the British officers came to Belgium with their men, and on the eve of battle attended a great ball.

Afterwards the men rejoined their regiments and the women drove out in their carriages to a vantage point from which to view the battle.

I am not suggesting that the wars we read about in history books were sporting or pleasant, or that all our ancestors settled their grievances without violence. Far from it. Our past is smeared with blood and cruelty. But I would emphasise that we are not moving away from, but instead into an increasingly brutal form of violence. The Nazis, probably Hitler himself, coined the term 'Total War'. In the past the majority of wars were not total, and indeed many situations which would have precipitated hostilities in our day were dealt with otherwise. Now all war is total war. Simply consider a very recent piece of evidence: the Russian annihilation of Grozny, capital of Chechnya.

I am merely making the point, once again, that war is not something that is intrinsic to our nature. It is something we did very happily without for millennia, but which we sadly then invented and are now in danger of being destroyed by.

In fact, it is during the past four or five hundred years that we have developed the social, economic and psychological structures that make war more probable and more ghastly.

The violent framework of modern (Western) society

Towards the end of the Middle Ages, that is to say from the latter part of the fifteenth to the middle of the sixteenth centuries, the foundations of contemporary Europe were being laid.

The principal of these was the emergence of something like the modern nation state, in which the ruler controlled centralised power. There had, of course, long been kings and grand dukes and other dignitaries who lorded it over a slice of Europe, lesser nobles and an anonymous mass of peasantry. But their fiefs were ramshackle agglomerations of which the Holy Roman Empire with its constantly shifting component parts was a prime example. It has been mocked as being neither holy nor Roman nor an empire, and is a good example of something in which the parts were more important than the whole. The island of England and France were locked into a long series of struggles for territory known as the Hundred Years War (1337-1453). Three hundred years before that Normans from France had invaded and taken over England and even earlier Scandinavians had colonised much of the two western islands; there was once a Norse kingdom which included both York and Dublin! So politics were somewhat fluid, but in general life went on without much change, whichever king was nominally in charge.

But gradually rulers became dissatisfied with their situation. If they wanted to go to war, which was not unusual if they felt they had a claim on a particular part of Europe, they had to petition their nobles to lend them men to do the fighting. Their position was not unlike that of the UN Secretary General who has to beg the member states to lend him troops for peace-keeping missions. Like President X or President

Y today, the nobles would often object. Even if they did not do so initially, they might call their men home in time to get the harvest in.

Moreover, although the kings had courtiers, they had no equivalent of a civil service; the affairs of the land were managed at a very local level by city councils and manorial courts. The king was in much the same position as were his nobles in running their own estates, the main difference being that his were larger and that he had more resources with which to run them.

But around this period, beginnings were made to establish regular national armies under the control of the king, together with the rudimentary exchequer and administrative machinery of an embryonic modern nation.

This administrative rationalisation both stimulated and was stimulated by the development of trade and banking. The Fugger Bank, the Giro Banco of Venice and the Exchange Bank of Amsterdam, which emerged in this period, were the forerunners of today's great financial institutions.

Science and hence technology, after a long period of stagnation, began to take off with the work of such as Galileo and Copernicus.

One of the most significant new developments was, however, of a different order: a new philosophy, even theology, of wealth deriving largely from the teachings of Calvin (1509–64), but spreading to other branches of the Christian Church and even to the Islamic world. These seemed to suggest that God showed his favour toward those elected (arbitrarily and not as a result of virtue) to join him in the next world, by showering on them material benefits in this one. Thus the idea that wealth and godliness were somehow interconnected began to take shape. It is with us to this day.

These five trends, the rise of the more or less centralised nation state, the development of national armed forces in place of soldiers levied from nobles, the growth of the banking system, expansion of science and technology, and not least the Calvinist philosophy, however distorted it may have been, began to interact in a variety of ways.

The armies served the nations in their efforts to expand and so to acquire new and greater national wealth with which to build even better armies and so increase their resources. The banks and financial institutions helped them in this respect, while the armies gave them some of the protection they needed to do this work. Both the business systems and also the political structures and principles within which they operated became more efficient in the important work of acquiring riches. The new religious philosophy contributed greatly by promoting the spirit of capitalism; as it did so the old prohibition (already somewhat attenuated) against usury and interest were discarded, which of course was greatly to the advantage of the new business enterprises. Finally the emergent technology, though not yet wedded to science, served by not only improving weaponry, but by facilitating the growth of fresh industries and improving old ones.

The interweaving of these, now with countless additional related elements, has grown ever more inextricable. As in an ecosystem, the smallest particle cannot be altered without affecting all the rest, a fact that exasperates reformers who believe that it is only necessary to remove one flaw for the system to work properly. One hears this argument about, for example, corruption and drugs. But why do people *want* to act corruptly; why do they *feel the need* for drugs? At once we plunge into deep, indeed unfathomable, waters.

This indissoluble concatenation of lethal ingredients has now, of course, spread far beyond Europe. It is in fact nearly universal since many of its practices and moralities, if they may so be called, have spread to countries like India and China whose culture is markedly different from that of the West where it developed.

In my own lifetime it has spread, it seems to me, like a virus into the remotest parts. I lived in the 1930s with what the anthropologists then insultingly called primitive peoples in the Arctic and the Middle East. I was impressed by the fact that the most respected men and women in the communities I knew were those who were known for generosity or piety, who were good story tellers or who best knew the tribal history, or were especially skilled in some trade or art. That these people were often among the poorest did not affect their standing; the rich might be envied but not respected for their wealth.

Now I find, however, that things have changed. Success is greatly respected and with success, its trappings: an air conditioned house, a Mercedes Benz, even in some most impoverished spot, a bicycle. People are now valued, as previously they were not, by external symptoms of achievement, rather than by personal skills and qualities.

Having said this, I must issue the sort of caveat that applies to much in this book. I am painting with a broad brush; you will all be able to think of exceptions and contradictions — so can I. But having been actively involved with the affairs of the world since my early manhood, I am convinced that the ruling values of most of the world's population are considerably more materialistic than they were.

Essentially this means that price and power are accepted as the measure of worth, rather than spiritual, intellectual, artistic, or moral qualities and values — unless any of these are unexpected money-spinners! Materialism, in fact, rules OK!

This combination of components, what we refer to proudly as Western civilisation, has contributed immeasurably to the state of the world as it is today: not just its technical mastery and high sophistication, but its wars, its callous neglect of the weak, its destruction of the environment. Above all it is a world in which a small proportion of us live in an affluent luxury unimaginable to my moderately well-off boyhood home, while the rest sink deeper into miserable indigence. In this alone, quite apart from the destruction of war, the distinguishing character of the world today is its violence.

Contemporary violence

The period of the Velvet Revolution in Eastern Europe — the breach of the Berlin wall, the collapse under firm nonviolent pressure of the regimes of East Germany and Czechoslovakia, the virtually unopposed changes in Hungary and Bulgaria, the turbulent but conclusive overthrow of the harsh Ceaucescu regime in Romania — was warmly greeted as a turning point in world affairs. Likewise the disintegration of the Soviet Union seemed to herald an age of democratic development and support for human rights. How deluded we were.

In a couple of years Yugoslavia had burst into flames and numerous new republics, many self-declared, had emerged in the Caucasus and in Central Asia with aggressive militancy. It is said that over thirty of these are engaged as I write (1995) in some level of angry conflict and that in the estimation of the Institute of Ethnology and Anthropology of the Russian Academy of Sciences, very many more conflicts are liable to break out.

The localised causes of these conflagrations vary greatly. There may be ancient rivalries, or populations forcibly relocated by Stalin and now restored may find their former homes occupied, or there may be religious differences, or there may be an urge to break links with Russia. But in several cases there is also a growth of criminality, and mafia-type organisations arise to defy or indeed take over the local administration. External intervention is treated with contempt. People who have so long been dominated by a now impotent outside authority are no longer ready to listen to toothless intimidation, advice or instructions whether from the Russian government or the European Union or the United Nations. Indeed, as the example of Chechnya shows, they will resist armed intervention with ferocity.

Meanwhile, many of the old wars drag on, rumbling, spluttering and occasionally flaring into incandescent fury in Sri Lanka, Cambodia, Somalia, Guatemala, Assam, Northern Burma, and

Kurdistan. In Afghanistan, having expelled the Russians, the Afghans turn on each other like maddened dogs. Everywhere the ordinary people, the Yous and the Is of the world, do their best to survive in increasingly intolerable conditions, their lands poisoned by defoliants, their villages razed, their fields uncultivated because they have been sown with land mines instead of seeds, their children dying prematurely because of malnourishment and lack of the most basic medical care. They huddle listless in huge camps, the beautiful people of the Chittagong Hill Tracts; the boat people who braved the seas and the pirates only to end in the prison cages of Hong Kong; Tamils, Zaireans, Kurds and endless others rot in the heartless detention centres of Fortress Europe.

The closest historical parallel to these chaotic struggles, especially in ex-Yugoslavia, is the Thirty Years War (1618-1648). It involved most countries of Western Europe, and great areas particularly of what is now Germany were ravaged and laid waste by the 'wolf strategy' — indiscriminate slaughter and destruction by the unpaid mercenaries who did much of the fighting.

Why? Why do we experience such periodical horrors? There is naturally always some reason for the mad rage, some old quarrel, some antique injustice to be cited as vindication for killing — and dying. But this is like excusing some serial killer because, like countless innocent others, he had an unhappy childhood. And why the unnecessary cruelty, the gloating torture, the incineration of women and children in churches, the rape and slow murder before a husband's eyes, the systematic victimisation of enemy prisoners? The last three or four decades perhaps offer some tentative explanation.

These things were not done in either World War I or II, except in the latter by Nazi-indoctrinated troops who had been taught that such as the Poles were not really human (but even so, why?). Some codes of conduct were retained, even in the most dreadful conditions. Wounded prisoners were treated, civilians were not intentionally molested except (except?) by impersonal mass bombing. The Geneva Convention was respected; but for the leaders in the wars we have just discussed, it might never have existed.

Disintegrated empires

However, the fact that comparable violence has occurred in both decolonised Africa and recently independent areas of the USSR may offer some hints of explanation.

One is that original groups of peoples had been disturbed; communities had been split; some had been moved away and then moved back to find their lands occupied (this happened to the Chechens and the Ingush); some had been placed under the control of others with whom they had little in common (this was the case with the Hutus, the cause of fearful conflict in Rwanda and Burundi); some had been joined incompatibly (the cause of the Nigerian civil war); some found themselves with new and disliked overlords (as did Abkhazians in Georgia). Another and more universal element was that they no longer knew their place in the world; they did not understand the nature of the particular entity to which they belonged. This has been the case with the Russians themselves. Those who disliked and feared communism could at least orient themselves in terms of these feelings of opposition. But, this source of hostility once removed, who were they, what should they work for? When much of our intellectual and emotional energy is expended negatively on dislike, there is little left over for imagination and creation.

My friends in Moscow are struck that their most sensitive acquaintances feel lost. This is really not surprising. For seventy years they had been told what to do and how to think. They had, in effect, been told that everything that was not compulsory was forbidden. They rebelled against this inwardly, but when the enemy vanished overnight, they were lost.

And this enemy had provided for them in a number of ways. It educated them, looked after their health, their housing and — at one level — their morals. Now they are on their own, without a guide. There is nothing to which they can either conform or express opposition. Small wonder if the vacuum is rapidly filled with criminal activities in Moscow, Osijek (which we shall discuss at length), or Chechnya.

Lastly, when the ruling power, communist or colonial, withdrew, so did many of the arrangements and institutions that provided security and identity — economic, political, military, and constitutional. Citizenship might be invalidated, as for some Serbs in Croatia. Church affiliation might be tainted, as in Rwanda, where many clergy took part in the bloodshed. Languages could cease to be officially recognised as legitimate means of communication, as in Bangladesh and Sri Lanka. People may be driven to the ultimate residual security, social, economic, psychological; to the family or clan, the tribal patois, the village collective, the fringe political movement, the neo-Nazi group, the shamanic revival — ultimately to the single alienated and autistic individual.

All of these constitute the soil from which grow the poisonous weeds of hatred and violence.

The lust for freedom

It is ironical that the sources of violence we have just been considering stem from a preceding source of violence: the lust for freedom and the liberation struggles, the wars against tyranny and oppression to which it leads. Sad to say, victory in these conflicts so often only leads to further suffering.

Western Europe is by no means free of liberation aspirations among peoples feeling themselves to be different culturally, linguistically or racially from the 'master' group. I admit to being affected by them, since my father's family comes from Scotland. Had I been there all my life I might well now be an ardent and angry nationalist. How much more so if I were a Basque in Spain or a Mayan in Guatemala.

But unlike much that we have been considering, the lust for freedom leads to a focused even if extreme violence. When its goals are achieved, however, new and confusing conflicts begin to erupt.

The violence of the city

If we who live in the great Western conurbations feel superior to the peoples of the North Caucasus or Africa for their involvement in 'tribal wars', we need only consider the condition of London or Manchester, Los Angeles or New York. Daily the media carry stories of atrocious crimes carried out on and by children, the teenage killer who stabs an old woman to death because 'he felt like it', contract killings, gang warfare, immigrant families incinerated in their homes by youths who have shoved petrol-soaked rags through the letterbox and dropped a lighted match on them, muggings and rapes by the hundred, young girls violated and then stabbed. A friend of mine was walking in front of the White House when a robber shot her companion in the head. Washington D.C. is known as the murder capital of the world — which is ironical as the President was doing his serious best to be the World's Chief of Police.

Then there is another dimension of violence: vandalism. In a way this is more frightening because of the lack of apparent motive. Many of the crimes against the person have at least a motive, however brutal or ignoble — lust, greed, anger, vanity, most of the deadly sins, in fact.

A few years ago my wife and I, taking a wrong turning, drove through an area of Manchester which was like a battle ground. The great apartment buildings, mostly tower blocks, were deserted and crumbling, ruined by their former tenants. Rank weeds grew in the empty spaces, pressing through the rubble of masonry, bits of plastic, the tin cans, all the detritus of dilapidation and poverty. I am not accusing the tenants of this waste land. I can imagine how foul it must have been to live there. I do accuse those, who no doubt include myself, responsible for creating the poverty, the ugliness and the impracticability of this and so many other areas. Indeed, I would like to stress the general point, which I think is highly relevant to any study of violence: that it is the measure of the moral and psychic health of the whole community. Nothing is more vain than to lay the blame on 'youth', or the 'permissive society', or on this political party or that. We are all responsible.

Within a few minutes walk from where we now live in south-east London recent months have shown much evidence of what is more individual than collective vandalism. I have mentioned the smashed bus shelter and telephone kiosk. The other day, walking in our local park, I noticed that a new bench, lovingly inscribed in someone's memory, is hacked to pieces; a row of young trees newly planted in the same place are broken. These are not serious crimes in the sense that murder is serious, but they are extremely serious in that they show a deep sickness, deeds of rage and despair at living in a world that offers no hope. They are not quite suicidal, but are certainly self-wounding. They are the acts which go against the interests of the actors, perpetrated within their own habitat: they use the bus shelter when it rains, they don't have a telephone and need the public one, they enjoy the use of the park.

All this amounts to an epidemic of individual violence for which there is as yet no cure. The police forces admit that they can do very little about it, that their traditional methods are largely ineffective. There are also, of course, what might be termed 'rational' crimes, committed for the conventional reasons of profit through robbery or fraud or in extreme cases, murder. But these are swamped by anarchic, pointless violence; the explosion of violence for no particular reason, the spontaneous knife-point mugging — the local area, where we buy our vegetables in the market, has the highest rate for this particular crime in the country.

(Let me here deal with the argument that since a great deal of violence is associated with drugs, especially with theft to maintain an addiction, it is not exactly purposeless. However, as I shall suggest a little later, the conditions that lead to the development of a drug habit are inextricably associated with those that foment violence).

The violence of the cities seems to be psychologically akin to the purposeless wars discussed earlier. Both are swathed in desperation and despair, both are suicidally self-destructive. Indeed I am half inclined not to separate them, but to say that the cities are already at war. But it is a mad war in which there is no true enemy except life.

Sources of violence in Africa

Africa, more perhaps than any other continent, seems to exemplify
the cruelty, the desperation, the immeasurable depth of human
suffering and above all the often pointless violence which typify our
age. Every type of disaster from famine to epidemic to genocide has
racked the unhappy continent. Exploitation and foreign mis-
management, though often well intentioned, have wrought havoc on
local economies and appropriate agricultural practices. When I first
lived and worked in Africa thirty-five years ago, it was a continent
(apart from such black spots as South Africa and the Portuguese
colonies) vibrant with hope and enthusiasm for the freedom which
had just arrived (as in Ghana, where we were) or was clearly around
the next bend. Now so much of it is haunted by the horrors it has
undergone and indeed is still suffering in Zaire, Rwanda, Burundi,
Liberia, Uganda. Perhaps I exaggerate but I fear only in the sense
that other areas are as badly off; indeed I do have firsthand experience of tragedies in other places (for example, the JVP insurrection
in Sri Lanka stands out in my experience as unspeakably loathsome;
the whole South of the country was turned into an abattoir — iron-
ically the North, where the 'real war' with the Tamil separatists was
proceeding, was at that time relatively peaceful). Nevertheless, the
travails of Africa constantly wring my heart.

Decolonisation

Fertile seeds of anarchic violence had already been sown before the
fairly rapid break-up of the colonial empires of Britain, France,
Belgium and other European countries. On the whole, this went very
smoothly with the exception of Portuguese Africa, where the metropolitan power long resisted calls for independence. The result was
that one devastating war (used originally as a proxy battleground by
the Cold War powers) was only in 1994 hopefully ending in Angola,
and one in Mozambique has only recently concluded.

But the change-over from dependency to independence involved
a readjustment which was perhaps as difficult psychologically as
politically. This was particularly the case in Africa, where the colonial territories seldom corresponded to any pre-existing social,
cultural, or political entity. This was not the case in 'French Indo-
China', which might well today have been very different, though
decolonised, but for the brutal absurdities of the war in Vietnam and
its continuing aftermath in Cambodia.

But in Africa the colonies, which mostly became free 'countries'
in the period from 1957 to the late 1960s, were different. Ghana,

where I lived with my family for three years, was composed of half a dozen tribes, each with their own language, and a large number of smaller ones, of which some had only a few hundred members, but which were ethnically and linguistically different from the others.

(I should explain that I use the word 'tribe' with some hesitation. It is a term we tend to employ in a slightly derogatory sense to imply a group of primitive, even barbaric, people. But in fact a tribe can be a nation in almost every way except that it hasn't a seat at the UN. It is a community of people of the same culture, having its own territory, legal and social principles, its history and traditions, its system of government and, as I have said, its own language. There are African tribes which have a larger population than do some European countries, such as Sweden and Finland).

Ghana is shaped like a rather attenuated rectangle, made up of the Ivory Coast on one side and Togo on the other, both French colonies though Togo had before World War I been a German territory. But on both these sides a large tribe was bisected by the frontier. Consequently half of one tribe were Togolese and half Ghanaian, and half the other Cote d'Ivorien and half Ghanaian. So who were Ghanaians? They were citizens of an area which had been allotted to Britain at a conference in Potsdam at the end of the last century where the would-be colonial powers drew lines on maps.

The case of Nigeria was even worse. It was much larger and the population much bigger. Half of them belonged to one of three very large tribes — the Hausa-Fulani, the Ibos and the Yoruba. But there were something like 700 languages and although most Nigerians seemed to be very good linguists, some used English as a lingua franca for communication. When Nigeria was given independence in 1960, I thought it was like telling, for example, France, Germany and Spain that they were now joined in a free democratic nation and should get on with the job of running it properly. This led to an atrocious civil war in which hundreds of thousands died. Ghana was more fortunate than Nigeria in not having oil which, poured on the politically troubled waters of Nigeria, fanned flames rather than calming them. But it shared the psychological problems of identity with Nigeria, Uganda, Eritrea, Zaire and twenty or so other African countries where there have been fearful conflicts.

Kenneth Kaunda, a wise and scholarly man who was the first president of Zambia and whom I had the good fortune to meet during the Zimbabwe war, told me that African societies were basically peaceful, but that the intrusion of Europe had often driven them to violence. The first and most vicious trauma was the two-hundred year long slave trade, which not only inflicted untold misery on countless individuals, but tore the fabric of African society into shreds, one group shamefully preying upon another to sell them into bondage.

There was then only a relatively short interval between the end of the slave trade early in the nineteenth century and the trickle of intrusion by traders and missionaries followed by colonial administrators which had turned into a flood well before its end.

Psychological wounds

My African friends have told me, as have African Americans, that these assaults and indignities not only caused enormous physical and emotional suffering, but created a deep sense of alienation. What sort of people are we, they thought, that we allowed these things to be done to us? When they call us stupid, ignorant and lazy niggers, they must be right; they are so much more powerful and capable. To save us from Hell they kindly give us their religion which tells us we were created for the purpose of hewing wood and drawing water. But the sense of inferiority and confusion was matched by a deep-seated anger.

When the colonial powers departed from most of Africa they left behind a system of law, administration and government based upon their own. Constitutional lawyers were appointed to draw up constitutions based on European models. The judges wore wigs and in the universities the students wore gowns. Ambivalently and uncertainly the Africans played at being white.

It was the same in the United States. One of my students told me that it had always been her ambition to be white in every way, save of course in colour. Her aims had been fulfilled: she lived in a predominantly white area, she taught in a white school where her two girls were also students. Then one day another black family came to live nearby and she told her daughters they should go and play with the newly arrived children. But they protested. 'Mommy', they said, 'they are coloured'. This suddenly made her realise what she had been doing to her identity, and she began to re-perceive herself as a black woman, one who exemplified the catch phrase of the day, 'black is beautiful'.

Of course Africa is a vast continent and also diverse. Until the Italian conquest, Ethiopia had never been a colony and was itself an empire, having overrun, subjugated and joined to itself several neighbouring peoples. Nor was Liberia a colony, but was nevertheless an extreme racist state in which the rulers were as black as the ruled, but were descended from slaves returned from America in the middle of the nineteenth century. The Muslim, largely Arabicised, north of the continent differed greatly in culture from black Africa to the south. The highlands of east and southern Africa where the whites came as settlers fared differently from the once lethally malarial West Africa where they came to do brief stints of work (or to die). And it made a difference whether the colonial rulers were British, French, or indeed any others. In British colonies the cultural centre was London; in French ones it was Paris. Although the nearly twenty French and British colonies were contiguous, they knew so little of each other that the American Quakers set up a centre with the sole purpose of bringing together Francophones and what a wag called Saxophones — who know nothing of each other and could not speak each others' colonial language, though they might speak the same African tongue. The telephone service exemplified the problems of communication; when in Lagos, capital of Nigeria, I wished to telephone to Cotonou, capital of what is now Benin, the call had to be routed to London, across to Paris and then south to Lagos, a total of some 8000 miles — Lagos and Cotonou being only 200 miles apart.

Not everyone, of course, had identity confusions. The majority perhaps were very little affected by the colonists and thought of them even less. But it was precisely those who held the keys to the future who suffered most. The well-schooled young men who led their countries to freedom were educated by dedicated teachers. If English, these tended to be cricket playing muscular Christians who instilled into them not only their knowledge of English literature and the classics, but their public school morality of sportsmanship, loyalty to the crown, and the general superiority of the British way. Even the great and at times virulent leader of African nationalism, Kwama Nkrumah, the first president of Ghana, could be almost sycophantic about the English and was personally devoted to the Queen. I used to meet him when I was a member of the Ghana University council, and we became friendly because we had daughters born on the same weekend and used to discuss their progress. He was charming and interesting, and his respect for the British officials who had helped Ghana move towards independence was genuine. But there was a tortured confusion in his emotions which I believe contributed to his downfall.

Such confusions led first to the acceptance of the guidance of abdicating European masters, later to their rejection and the establishment of one-party states rather than democratic parliaments on a European model. Later, all too often, came war.

The toll of violence

Since about 1960 around twenty-five wars have been fought, or are still being fought, in Africa. Some were wars against an oppressive and alien government in, for example, Angola, South Africa, Mozambique, Kenya, Zimbabwe, Namibia, Guinea Bissau, Eritrea. But the majority of the rest have been confused internal struggles for no easily definable purpose, periods of blundering carnage during which nothing was gained and a great deal lost.

In 1991 I attended in Namibia a workshop on 'Healing the Wounds of War in Africa'. Women and men from eleven countries which had suffered serious wars attended, about thirty in all. Most were from the nations concerned; I was there because I had been involved in two wars, the civil war in Nigeria and the independence struggle in Zimbabwe. I think we were all deeply depressed by what we heard. We obviously knew much about the horrors of the individual countries we were familiar with, but the cumulative effect of what we were learning overwhelmed us.

We not only learned about the killings and the torture, but the shattering of social relations and consequently the decay of agriculture, the hunger, the unemployment, the armies of small boys whose only skill was slaughter from which they had no social morality to deter them. And above this, the dark shadow of AIDS exacting a toll of death, which every government did its best to conceal.

The de-development of Africa

Finally we have learned, and I have since learned much more, about the disastrous interventions of agencies such as the International Monetary Fund which, in the name of building a sound economy, has diverted resources from providing minimal satisfaction of basic human needs, 'structural adjustment'. As a result of this type of policy, not only in Africa, but also in the USA, Britain and other 'developed' societies, standards of educational provision, nutrition, health care and hence of health and life expectancy are declining among the poor, while the proportion of the absolutely poor is increasing.

The violence of the state

We know that the modern state came into existence partly to enable the mediaeval and post mediaeval monarch to exercise more centralised control and to wage war more efficiently. However benign the king or queen might have been, they thus gained greater power to exercise violence, and indeed made use of it.

Today there are virtually no absolute monarchies. They have been replaced by presidents heading republics or by constitutional monarchs, figureheads presumed useful to the countries concerned. Such monarchs 'rule' in Britain, Sweden and a few other European countries. But the governments of these heads of state, monarchical or not, retain the capacity to go to war, or to act violently in other ways, such as oppressing their own people or some of them.

In some, this power is considerably curtailed by a strongly democratic constitution, but in others it has been taken over absolutely by an authoritarian government or a dictator. At the moment, about one third of the member states of the UN have such regimes. On the other hand, only a handful — perhaps twenty, mostly in Western Europe — have truly democratic governments. By that, I mean governments which are genuinely responsive to the desire of all the people for a good society, the civil society; a society in which no groups of people such as the poor or immigrants are marginalised; good health care, education and housing are available to all; justice is administered impartially; the police are not repressive; labour is respected and properly employed, not casualised; local institutions through which the citizens can rule local affairs and influence the legislature are valued and encouraged. Above all, it is a society in which citizenship is honoured as a proud status in which both rights and responsibilities are balanced to the advantage of both state and individuals.

In even the most democratically advanced countries there are some failings in certain of these respects. We are all, I suppose, conscious of the flaws in our own social environment. I cannot be proud, though I would like to be, of the current state of England (I say England rather than Britain, because I believe that the failings that affect me most come particularly from the contributions of English

traditions and culture, rather than those of Scotland or Wales — I
leave out Northern Ireland because of its controversial position).

Our revolution, the earliest and least bloody of European revolu-
tions was, perhaps for this reason, never quite completed. The residue
of monarchical power is still firmly embedded, not so much of course
in the mainly symbolic royal family, as in the derived network of institutions — the Church of England, the mandarinate of senior civil
servants, the quango membership, the armed services, landowners, the
institutions of City and Treasury, the boards of businesses, and the
public schools which man (the word is appropriate) these bodies. In
the late 1940s after the upheaval of the war, and to some extent in the
1970s, this crust of unplanned but almost instinctual control was
cracked. We became a nation of citizens for the first time.

But from 1979 onwards, not only were most of the gains since
1945 steadily eroded, but more ancient bulwarks of democratic citizenship were stormed and broken down: the local councils of city
and county. When I was first a voter, the successful candidates for
seats on such councils were not so much chosen for their political
party as because they were considered to be good and sensible
women and men. However, when these bodies became a political
arena, they also became a potential threat to the Conservative hege-
mony and their powers were greatly reduced by Westminster. The
government even went to the shameful lengths of dissolving the
Greater London Council, leaving London the only capital city in
Europe, I believe, without its own governing body.

The motive for this retrogression is, of course, the New Right's
ideology of the market. 'There is no such thing as society', Mrs
Thatcher proclaimed; leave everything to the market and all will be
well. So the government must divest itself of all financial obligations
(so far as is politically feasible) to care for such things as health,
education and housing (hence the disastrous policy of selling off
council houses which has left so many people homeless), and
ridding itself of responsibility for water, the post office, and other
amenities essential to the well-being of the people, and even some
prisons and related services. (It might be said that communist
regimes did take responsibility for all these and other measures
designed to benefit the people, thus qualifying for the description of
good societies; but no society that served this purpose by killing,
transporting, and imprisoning in labour camps vast numbers of its
people could possibly be called good).

The government following such policies energetically will be left
with responsibility for foreign relations, the armed services, the intel-

ligence agencies and, perhaps above all, the legislative and monetary policies, and powers to enhance and protect the free operations of the market.

As has become only too obvious, however, the market forces do not operate to the benefit of us all. There are two main reasons for this. The first is that the market ideology is one of intense individualism; there is no wider community to which we need or indeed should feel responsibility, and our only obligation is to operate freely and vigorously in the market. The second reason is that we do so in the context of a society (*pace* Mrs Thatcher) that has what I call a traditional crust. This crust is now strengthened, its rifts repaired, by members recruited from the City and financial houses who have been drawn by the lack of restraints and the opportunity. For these, the last decade and a half have on the whole been years of great profit. Not so for those below the crust, particularly those thrown out of work by the government policy of neglecting industry (except the arms industry) and whose welfare benefits have been whittled away; these, of course, are the new underclass. So much for the cosy governmental myth of a share owning democracy.

In fact, the owning of shares only widens the split between those who have something and those who have less than nothing, only debts and unmet needs. The nation's well-being will not be promoted by the ownership of shares, but by creating the conditions in which everyone has not only a share, but a stake (see Bibliography, Will Hutton's *The State We're In*) in the growth of a vital *new* society, one in which all can play an enthusiastic part, a part which is truly *nonviolent*.

At the moment, it must be stressed that we in Britain live in a violent and in many ways cruel society. It is not simply that there are some unfortunate people who have had bad luck. It is that a large part of our consciously devised national social and economic policy, grafted onto a traditionally class-ridden society, does active harm; it tends to diminish human potential. Our politicians have no doubt not planned this with intent to do damage, but they see what is happening and are insufficiently concerned to change their policies; ideology apparently matters more to them than the lives which are being hurt by it.

The idea of Britain as violent (apart from the violence of the streets which is known and deplored) may seem strange. Is the country not benign compared with many other countries? Yes, indeed. But it is important to realise that even in predominantly gentle societies there may be structural elements potentially making for violence, factors that can be accentuated very swiftly in certain circumstances. Only by recognising them can we take steps to prevent their escalation, or to alter them.

Global militarism and violence

Two facts epitomise the extent of the world's militarism. The leaders of the world's great peace movement, the United Nations, the five permanent members of the Security Council, not only are the world's five nuclear powers, but also the largest manufacturers and exporters of arms. A fine example!

The years after the First World War saw serious and, for a while, promising attempts at disarmament, but after the second the enmity between the USSR and the rest of the Allies made comparable efforts impossible. On the contrary, in fact. As each side strove to gain strategic allies in various parts of the world to fight its proxy wars and to exclude its enemies, the merchants of death, as former generations aptly called them, prospered greatly.

In a way this was not difficult. The cult of militarism was by no means new. In Europe there had been for centuries a tradition of warrior kings — Charlemagne, Frederick the Second, Gustavus Adolphus, Henry V — and even women — Elizabeth I and Catherine the Great — owed their repute largely to success in war and diplomacy.

In our own times General Franco, not as king of course, but as President of Spain, continued the tradition of soldier-ruler. He set an example to the countless generals who since have staged military coups and then clung to power. To do him justice, Franco did not have the hypocrisy to promise free elections which were never held or, if held, invalidated if the results were not to his liking. Other president/generals however, such as those of Nigeria and Burma, have not been so scrupulous.

To be fair again, I should mention another general, Dwight D. Eisenhower, who not only made no attempt to stick in office unconstitutionally, but was well aware of militaristic dangers. He went so far against the interests of his caste as to warn against what he called, coining an apt phrase now in universal usage, the military-industrial complex. To his honour he did this long before many of us recognised the danger of such establishments.

The long tradition of involvement of royalty and rulers with the army has given the armed forces almost universally a special standing in the state. Most great official occasions are accompanied by some form of military display, ranging from the terrifying parade of weapons which graced (or disgraced) May Day celebrations in the Red Square in Moscow, to the military band or march past of the Territorial Army on civic occasions in Britain. Most members of the British royal family have had some military training and hold such positions as colonel-in-chief of a regiment; the relevant uniforms are often worn by them. This is partly, but by no means entirely, a picturesque survival. Most of us accept it, as we accepted the fact that a son of the Queen fought in the Falklands War, or that his great uncle, then Prince of Wales, fought and was decorated in World War I. A good example of patriotism for all of us.

So there is a solid and ancient base for the booming militarism of today. The Cold War has built vast tower blocks, so to speak, on this foundation. Both sides poured weapons (improved models after the experience of the preceding hot war) into potential allies or bases in the Third World, especially those like Angola or Ethiopia where there was actual conflict in progress.

A little later the arms trade was further boosted by decolonisation. In places where the colonial powers were trying to hang on, there was a great demand for weapons, both 'legitimately' by the colonialists and by the liberation forces. Soon large areas of Asia and Africa were awash with arms.

The situation was slightly different in Latin America, there being hardly any colonists to evict, but in most countries there was oppression. In a world where consciousness of injustice was awakening, and as people realised from examples elsewhere that change can occur, this led to violence. During the last few decades there have been guerrilla movements or uprisings in most American countries south of the United States. Here too was a good market for arms. I am sometimes asked how all these rebel groups, operating clandestinely, can get their supplies of arms; certainly not directly from official suppliers in, for example, Britain? No. I can only say that those who run this unofficial aspect of the arms trade are, like drug dealers, ubiquitous, experienced, cunning and unscrupulous.

The next, and to my mind most tragic, stage is the 'legitimate' sale of arms to countries which have won their independence (with or without fighting) and now want to establish themselves as nation states with all the trimmings. These include not only a UN seat but, as almost top priority, their own armed services. The possession of the latest hi-tech weapons all too soon becomes a competitive status symbol. I still find it a little hard to account for this logically. In Africa, where the greatest number of new countries came into existence within a short period from the later 1950s to the mid 1960s, there was virtually no possible external threat. Later, as the pressures of Cold War manoeuvring mounted and as internal dissention grew, it could be understood. And of course, as soon as one state arms, its neighbours feel threatened and follow suit. But I believe that at the outset they were deluded by the ancient myth put about by their former colonial power that nationhood and military strength are inseparable.

It is a belief that becomes true if we believe it. Even as Kwame Nkrumah believed it. Yet he was the apostle of African unity, which could have been at least partially achieved if the departing, but economically present, powers had refrained from interference, and if their 'aid' packages had not been tied with lethal strings.

But as the poor nations militarised themselves, so they rendered themselves liable to that most deadly of constitutional diseases, the military coup. Virtually every militarily entrenched government (and indeed some others) has increased its military budget at the expense of those for health and education, reduced the freedom of its people, and frequently attacked its neighbours.

Optimists hoped that when the Wall came down and the Cold War ended, the world would be demilitarised. There have, in fact, been a few nods in that direction, but mostly we have been disappointed. We had, perhaps, forgotten how deeply the military-industrial complex had become embedded, not only in the economy but also in our culture, particularly that of the West. It was thought that once there was no more enemy, either communist or capitalist, we could relax. But no. The busy search is on for new enemies and for new and craftier weapons to fight them with. Our protective agents are glancing, slit eyed, at the threat of Muslim extremists, of new nuclear powers (to whom we have probably supplied the technical know-how and the equipment), of jealous forces in the South which resent the dominance of the North. But the military-industrial complex and their political dupes won't let us be taken unawares, or allow their profits to decline.

But primarily, perhaps, it is our hard-headed but of course only realistic, never hard-hearted, mandarins in Whitehall, and their equivalents in the Champs-Elysées, the Kremlin and elsewhere who know how much the trade was worth. Mrs Thatcher certainly set the scene in Britain. She allowed (encouraged?) other aspects of British industry to run down, but cosseted the arms factories and, as is well known, promoted the sale of British manufactured arms and equipment wherever she could.

The British argument is that this is not only profitable, but also provides jobs. But the now very much weakened civilian industry could have provided more jobs, while the arms factories could also have been converted to civilian uses. The economic issue is equally specious for other reasons. Any gain is short-lived because to build for destructive rather than constructive purposes does nothing for the development of either society or economy, and merely wastes an enormous amount of scientific and technological brain power.

Bearing all this in mind, it is easy to recognise the implacable militarism of our world. The lunatic wars, the desperation, alienation and despair are fed by the factories of the West, nourishing our over-fed society with the flesh and blood of the hungry. Our predatory policies of profit at any price have richly manured the field in which the seeds of future ethnic cleansing, cruelty and conflict may grow.

This has frequently happened in an indirect fashion. There is, however, a clear connection between militarism, environmental degradation and poverty. Taking the latter first, poverty often forces the poor to make demands on the environment through overcropping and deforestation, which in turn lead to serious environmental damage leading later to famine and greater poverty. At the same time, the cost of militarisation reduces the amount available for development which would alleviate poverty and reduce over-use of the environment. In addition, military activity — let alone war — is both entirely nonproductive and highly polluting.

The interaction of all these factors tends greatly to increase local tensions and to heighten the likelihood of conflict. Thus one effect of militarisation is to increase the probability that yet more militarisation may be felt to be necessary; one of the vicious circles so prevalent in times of stress and violence.

Those who may be interested in a few statistical facts to illustrate this chapter may like to look at the next paragraphs; otherwise I suggest they turn to the next chapter.

Figures of war

The developed nations of the world spend enough on arms annually to feed the 2 billion poorest people in the world for the same period. Although in 1990 they provided $56 billion in aid to the poorest countries, they also sold them $36 billion in weaponry — and significantly it is in these countries that most of the armed conflicts occur; if they were to halve their military expenditure, they could provide health care that would save 10 million lives a year.

A great deal of this violence occurs in nations having a military-controlled government. Of 112 developing countries, 51 became independent after 1959. The following year 26 were under some sort of military regime. By 1992 the number had risen to 61. In all but two of these countries the most extreme sorts of oppressive violence are practised — torture, political killings, disappearances. In most cases this seems to be officially condoned.

In other developing countries under military government, 62 per cent exercise extreme violence on the civilian population. In those not under military government 24 per cent do so.

Since it is known that a great majority of all armed conflicts are within the nation, civil wars, and that a high proportion of these are a response to repression, the above statistics would suggest that countries under military governments would be more prone to war than are others. This is indeed the case. In the thirty-three year period up to 1992 they have on average suffered more than six times as many years of war.

According to the statistics I have been quoting, in 1992 there were 29 full scale wars with the highest annual total of deaths in seventeen years (another equally reliable count put the number at 32). At that time there were probably about 70 lesser but lethal conflicts and since then more have broken out than concluded.

Since 1945 there have been 149 wars having a total of 23 million fatal casualties, of whom well over 60 per cent were civilian — this proportion has risen, of recent years, to nearly 90 per cent.

The speed of change

How did it all start? We have identified decolonisation and the end of the Soviet empire as one key factor. This obviously does not affect the cities of America and Western Europe. However, what is significant about that was the relatively sudden and rapid change involved. And certainly this is something that Europe and the Americas and other 'developed' areas have experienced to the full. Indeed, the greater the 'development' the greater and more rapid the change brought about by an amazing and continuous revolution in technology.

A few years ago I read Oliver Goldsmith's *The Vicar of Wakefield* for the first time. It was written in the middle of the eighteenth century, but the general quality of the rural life it depicted was more similar to what I had experienced as a boy in the 1920s, than the life of the 1920s resembled that of the 1970s. There had, in fact, been more change in fifty years than in the previous two hundred and fifty. The setting of my own life has changed comparably. I was brought up in a large house with a beautiful garden, but without running water, central heating, gas, or electricity, and without radio, telephone, car or any of the innumerable gadgets by which I am now surrounded, certainly without the computer with which I am writing these words. But we did have servants and a gardener, and we had a pony and trap with which to drive to the market five miles away, and to the station. Now I live in a small house in south-east London. We have no servants or gardener and do all our own work, except that we rely on the help of a friend who is glad to earn a little as a handyman. But electricity, gas and technology come to our aid and we can't complain of leading a hard life.

Certainly the wealthy world has been transformed since 1945 by the jet engine, the silicon chip, antibiotics, television and a host of significant derivatives of these and other technological innovations which have revolutionised economies, communications and social relations. A much larger proportion of the population than the two or three per cent of fabulously wealthy people are what may be called seriously rich; a much larger proportion also are now miserably poor,

and usually unemployed. Few big towns are without their cohorts of
beggars and the homeless sleeping in shop doorways.

The changes in lifestyle, whether achieved or thrust upon us, are
associated with changes in patterns of relationships. Marriages, for
example, are much less likely than before to last beyond a few years.
I am not making a moral point here, but stating a fact which has
considerable implications for the character of society. Technical
changes have also affected employment. Apart from the fact that
automation has devoured countless jobs, whole categories of occupation have virtually disappeared. During the last century when the
railway and then the car replaced the horse drawn stage coach, a
complete class of worker concerned to feed, groom and in general to
look after the horses simply disappeared. The farmers and merchants
who supplied the fodder suffered likewise. They were of course
replaced functionally by garages, the suppliers of gasoline, and
mechanics; by railway workers, porters and linesmen. However,
these tended to be different sorts of people with different types of
connection. One form of occupation which has been replaced, save
in the homes of the very rich, is the domestic servant. She or he is
replaced by the vacuum cleaner, the washing machine, the dish
washer and the food processor. Similarly the carpenter or other
skilled artisan has been replaced by the DIY shop.

And so on. Almost everyone is now middle class, except the very
poor, who are no longer lower class, but an underclass without any
standing in society.

Although industrialisation increased greatly during the second half
of the last century, change in general was gradual since the end of the
Middle Ages. The concatenation of the elements of the modern state
proceeded in a leisurely fashion. In Europe as a whole during this
period, society evolved in association with the evolution of moral attitudes and behaviourial patterns. As in most fairly static societies,
these tended to be mutually supporting in the sense that what was
morally acceptable was also socially expedient. (Please note that I am
not saying this is always desirable; what is considered morally laudable is not necessarily just or fair. The stability which follows from a
congruence of the two can also be corrupt and tyrannical).

But the great changes of the last five decades have disrupted the
balance. The changes have been too rapid for the evolution of an
appropriate social morality. This means, amongst other things, that
the checks on criminal or anti-social behaviour lose much of their
force. Instead of being condemned as 'bad', they are frequently characterised as enterprising or ingenious, as evidence of keen business

practice or as youthful high spirits — or casually dismissed as nothing worth mentioning.

The sixties and the seventies

The twentieth century has been one of extraordinary transformation, especially its second half. Not only has it seen the technological revolution and the end of the great imperia, but an increasingly global economy that transcends frontiers, and the establishment of vast international agencies. These all combine to bring about unprecedented social change and upheaval, the collapse of ancient moral imperatives, and a spate of shifting standards on everything from sexual behaviour to aesthetics and politics.

A glance at the post-war decades during which most of these transformations were occurring may show more clearly how these movements relate to the violence which we are examining.

For the nations which had been involved in World War II, the late 1940s and the 50s were a period of hope and of reconstruction. The governments of both the United States and the United Kingdom were vigorous and humane, eager to break away from a past which had brought two wars and the depression of the 1930s. In Britain particularly it seemed as if a new era of justice and equal opportunity was at hand.

The 1960s and early 1970s constituted the most enlightening period of my life. Having been raised in a solid upper middle class literary and academic atmosphere my opinions were decent, liberal and conventional. They were, however, turned upside down by my students. I learned from them that my teaching style, though affable, was formal, selfish, and took insufficient account of their interests and abilities. I learned from those of them who had been in the Peace Corps (I was teaching in America) much more than I had learned in several years in Asia and Africa, about the neo-colonial relationship through which the rich countries dominated and exploited the poor ones just as effectively as they had done as colonial rulers, and with less trouble. I learned from my women friends how I assumed masculine superiority in many ways. I learned from my black friends (at least we became friends in the process) that though I had many African and Asian intimates, I had mentally transformed them into honourary whites. And in the process of learning these things, it was I who began to be transformed.

Over and beyond all these secular, as it were, issues, was one much more profound. My mentors, and I with them, began to realise that our perception of ultimate realities was flawed or limited. There

was something we were missing and we sought it in the Vedanta, the
Gnostic Gospels, Mahayana Buddhism, Native American religion,
the Sufis, the fourteenth-century European mystics. We sought it in
our own churches and I recall how our somewhat staid Quaker
meeting became full of wild young people with long hair and
flashing eyes who had drunk the milk of the sixties paradise.
Unfortunately many also sought it in drugs. But thought these
might offer a foretaste of illumination which could have been
followed up by safer and more systematic means, they also led to
damaging and disastrous addictions. And there were others whose
spiritual quest led them to superficiality and silliness.

On the whole, however, it was period of great enlightenment and
opportunity. We do wrong to calumniate it because of excesses
which were no more extreme than those of enthusiasts for any other
cause, and a lot less dangerous than many.

The late 1970s and the 1980s saw a dramatic reversal of the mood
of the sixties. The atmosphere of idealism, the selfless quest for
justice, the spiritual awareness, were swamped by a cynical materialism. It was during this period that many of the governments which
had espoused liberal and humane welfare policies — for example
New Zealand, a pioneer in state health provision — were replaced
by those with a much harsher economic policy. Unemployment rose,
the gap between rich and poor grew ever wider, critics of the new
approach — clergy or social workers, for example, who deplored the
miseries of the poor — were violently attacked by spokeswomen and
men of the administrations concerned.

I tried to catch the tenor of such diatribes in the following lines
(from a longer poem):

> Upon the mob they foist their truth:
> 'The proof of virtue lies in wealth,
> it shows your spiritual health,
> seek it without the slightest ruth.
>
> 'If people stop you with their cries,
> eg. the poor or unemployed,
> fling them aside, they have enjoyed -
> and wasted — opportunities.
>
> 'Now it is time they paid the price
> for their improvidence, and worked
> at useful jobs they've always shirked.
> Poverty is the fruit of vice.
>
> 'The churches talk a lot of shit:
> loving your neighbour, all that crap.

> Society is just a trap:
> the socialists invented it
>
> 'to slow our dedicated quest
> for profit. It's a lonely search;
> just leave the others in the lurch.
> Best motto: BUGGER ALL THE REST'.

But to be honest, although it is tempting to blame particular politicians for what goes wrong, it is somewhat unfair. Because of the close interconnections of the world economic structure, no single system can be fully autonomous in framing its policy.

Now, in the nineties, we can begin to count the cost of the convulsive changes of the last three decades. The humanitarian dreams are shattered and discarded, the welfare provisions mere skeletons of what they were. Even the social democracy of the Swedes has suffered sorely. New Zealand, once the model of the welfare state, has now abandoned it completely and has moreover one of the highest crime rates in the world. Both education and health services in Britain have been viciously mauled. Unemployment is a global phenomenon.

There are not so many major wars as there were ten to fifteen years ago; these were mostly spawned by great power rivalry, but there are now very many more vicious small ones. There are hopes of peace in a few places, but progress is slow, the track precarious and the Gadarene slope is steep, slippery and crowded. And meanwhile the carnage continues unabated in Cambodia, Afghanistan, Liberia, the former Yugoslavia. And so on and on, as though the UN, the European Union, the Organisation of African Unity had never existed. The surface of human society is covered with pustules of violence, on large scale and small. But all of these are merely the bloody hilt of a knife whose blade deeply penetrates the lives of each one of us; slicing into hearts, perhaps, certainly into our civilisation. I sense it every night when I lock up the house; I also know that if an entry were forced, I should give the burglar what he wanted or risk being knifed.

The second half of the 1990s, a decade which started so well and deteriorated so rapidly, looms enigmatically before us. But we have now perhaps enough evidence to understand the nature of the all-pervasive violence.

The digging stick parable

I have been told a story, possibly a legend, certainly a parable, which describes the effects that change may have.

There was an Australian aboriginal group in the northern part of the country, protected from direct contact with farmers and other white Australians by an area of almost impenetrably swampy country. For what little cultivation they carried out, they used a digging stick. This, like all their tools, was not just a useful implement, but something of ritual value. It had to be made and used in a way and at a time sanctioned by the sacred traditions of the people. Its use, therefore, not only had practical importance, but kept vividly alive in the minds of the Aborigines the beliefs and practices which held them together as a group. But it also ensured that they did the right thing at the right time agriculturally. Things were not, of course, planned like this. It just happened that this functional coincidence had developed over a long period of time.

Moreover, the ritual significance of the digging stick was a part of the set of interwoven relationships and activities concerning sexual behaviour, social responsibility, hunting and the upbringing of children. This pattern of interdependent acts and relationships constituted the law, or the religion, upon which the group's cohesion depended.

But one day, somehow or other, some spades were introduced into the group. The men experimented gingerly with them, but found that they were much more efficient than the digging sticks. Eventually they all came to use them. Naturally, however, since the spades were not the sticks , they neglected the ritual. Digging was now just a manual activity, not a sacred (if useful) act. But since the ritual was a part of a totality, the totality was damaged; the unity for which the ritual had stood was now lost.

Now everybody began to neglect the old, hallowed rules. The cohesion of the group was lost. The people became listless and confused. For example, when they hunted kangaroos they no longer respected their prey, but wantonly killed, as a sport, more than they needed. Thus they depleted the flock and came, themselves, to be hungry.

Soon individuals began to drift off, demoralised and unhappy. They wandered to the towns or the farms, where they learned to drink or steal. And some of them became very angry and violent.

Perhaps this breaking of the mould of custom opened up a vast range of new possibilities for their development. However, since everyone in their community was suffering from the same anomie, there was no one to tell them what to do.

How things happen

The things we have been discussing are all interrelated, just as the digging sticks and their rituals are connected with the rituals of birth, marriage and death. The spread of senseless violence, the emergence of under classes, the increasing gap between rich and poor, alienation and despair — all are interwoven, all are part of the seamless and in many parts ugly tapestry of the existence of the human family. Unless we understand this and have some idea of how it comes about, we have no way of making the pattern more harmonious. If we just tinker with the parts, anything we manage to achieve will be limited and temporary; any small local improvement will soon be infected and nullified by the degenerating whole.

On the level of the human mind, our mind, the Three Poisons are just as much connected, inseparably interdependent, both with each other and with low awareness. So they are also with the false identity or ego.

These interdependencies follow through into our social — indeed our global — existence. For example, the anger arising out of the three poisons intrudes into our social relations, while our greed affects our economic life, and indeed other aspects of our behaviour. There is certainly an interface, or rather an interpenetration, of these inner and outer realms. Over the ages our needs and greeds have encouraged the establishment of institutions related to their satisfaction — banks, stock exchanges, business enterprises of all sorts. Our angers, ambitions and again greeds have, on the large scale, contributed to the institutions of war — the armed forces, staff colleges, intelligence agencies, defence industries and the like.

I am not saying, however, that these things *cause* each other. What they do is to create together the conditions in which it is possible for them to exist. We are talking about enormous systems, systems both within and outside our bodies, which are in constant interaction. It is simplistic to assert that one event brings about another. To take a very obvious example: my wife and I have a daughter; neither of us is the cause of her existence, but together we established the conditions necessary for it to be possible.

An infinitely more complex example is, for instance, the ecology of a rainforest; trees, creepers, insects, animals, plants, bacteria — including, paradoxically, the ones which prey upon each other — together make each others' lives possible.

To understand things in this light, not as separate, nor as causing each other, but as *co-arising,* is the essence of non-dualism. The dualist separates things — God and his creation, good and bad, right and wrong, you and me, the victim and the attacker.

Non-dualism sees reality as a *system,* or rather a vast system of interlocking systems — in our minds, our bodies, in the whole world around us, and extending — though there is little we can do about it

— into the universe; the great All or One of which we and our own set of sub-systems — physiological, intellectual, emotional — form a part.

This mode of understanding things and how they happen, even if our understanding is partial, without doubt affects our possibility of changing them. Belief in straightforward causation might lead us to think that, for instance, punishment deterred crime and the harsher the punishment the greater the deterrent. But we know that this is not the case; criminal acts (or whatever a particular age considers criminal acts) are the product of a combination of innumerable factors — social, psychological, economic, ideological; and the factors that bring about behaviourial changes are all equally complex.

A linear cause-and-effect approach is clearly not in accord with the reality of our interconnectedness, nor indeed with the reality of the systems approach which is basic to ecology and all other sciences.

Culpability

We usually try, when we are upset or angry, to identify who or what is responsible. This simplifies things — and is also a let-out for us. However, if we really understand the way things happen, we cannot allow ourselves the indulgence of blaming particular people, whether such individuals as Hitler, Stalin or Mao (whom I admit I used to think of as a kindly old gentleman bobbing around in the Yangtze), or lesser but equally monstrous tyrants such as Idi Amin or Papa Doc or self-styled Emperor Bokassa. Nor can we blame circumstances such as war, famine or pestilence.

We cannot attribute the world's violence to the evil, weakness or stupidity of some particular group. We cannot even attribute it to the USA which has laid waste so much of the Third World with its defoliants and pesticides, gutted it with agribusiness, and supported the most loathsome regimes to satisfy its greedy paranoia. Or to the communists who slaughtered their own people and poisoned their own lands to create happiness. Or the right-wing well-heeled Christian fundamentalists who have changed a religion of love to one of hate. Or the Islamic militants who shoot prostitutes and cut off the hands of thieves. Or to all bigots of any faith, political, economic or religious. Or the multinationals, whose rapacious tentacles reach throughout the world. Or the members of the United Nations who blithely sign conventions on human rights and then go home to flout them. But all of these, and an infinity of others, together constitute the base of everything that is. And that includes you and me.

Determinism and responsibility

A further issue should be considered at this point: determinism. It could be argued that the more we understand the multiplicity of issues that converge to produce a particular event, the more we will see that it was determined, that it could not have been otherwise. Thus Newtonian cosmology reveals a predictable universe in which, for example, the advent of a comet or eclipse can be foretold to the second. But this predictability does not apply to everything. Heisenberg's uncertainty theorem shows why we cannot measure with precision both the position and the momentum of an atomic particle. In an atomic field of force each element is in constant and therefore unpredictable interaction with every other; even all the apparently solid and immutable objects around us, stones and tables and mountains are forever changing.

Constant change is certainly the case, as indeed we have already seen, with human beings. There is, however, an argument against the application of any sort of equivalent to the uncertainty principle to human beings; the principle of *karma*.

This is considered by some as a kind of retributive justice for ill-doing in this or previous lives. But this is incorrect. The true meaning is the very obvious one, namely *that we are affected by everything we do, say, or think*. We are unquestionably the product of our mental and physical actions, both good and bad, desirable and undesirable. There is no need to posit earlier lives; the evidence of our past is always with us.

However, we have a widely ranging consciousness with considerable powers of choice and decision. These too are indeed subject to *karma,* to the inertia of custom and habit and fixed attitude; but we are also able to do something about them. And countless millions do so with more or less effect. They do so by religious exercises, by meditation, by psychotherapy, by sorrow for wrong doing and by reparation, and simply by becoming more aware, and thinking things out.

In particular, by looking at things with genuine realism. Through understanding what things are and how they happen, people discover the right action to take in order to affect the system. In this way they can escape the psychic or spiritual determinism of *karma* — or whatever we like to call this very natural phenomenon.

It is very important to recognise that, in however limited a way, we are not helpless in the face of problems that seem dauntingly enormous. The first encouragement is to realise that we are actually a part of every obstacle to harmony and so can do something about it. Just as a host of cells and molecules take effective healing action when we scratch ourselves, so we as individuals can always make some positive contribution to the removal of any obstacle. It is equally important to recognise that being a part of the obstacle does not disqualify us from acting; we have no 'karmic disability'. Moreover, because we are aware that we are part of it, we have power to act effectively.

Diagnostics

There is no reason to think that violence of the sort we have been considering is all new. There have always been cruelty and vandalism and crazily pointless quarrels, feuds and wars. What is different now is the global scale, the interrelatedness, the cross-fertilisation and copy-cat brutalities. In the past when the incidents were fewer and the world less closely interconnected, it might have been easier to isolate them and cope with them diplomatically or militarily or by policing; now there seems to be a hydra-headed monster that is out of control, self-nourishing.

If, as seems probable (rather than just possible), the more legitimate grounds for conflict increase — conflicts connected with resources and the environment, with growing inequalities, with the consequent arms races — then no doubt the less rational expressions of conflict will also proliferate: violence for any cause encourages yet more violence.

Indeed, we have to act quickly if we are to prevent the global situation becoming entirely out of control. But what is this anarchic and aimless violence that threatens so much and so many?

Alienation

A short and preliminary definition would be that it represent an *alienation* from our common humanity. I strongly stress *common* humanity, because the other side of the coin may be an intense involvement with a particular branch of our race which has set itself against all others, as have done certain religious cults, political sects, or national or tribal groups. Equally it may be an individual rather than a group matter, one involving a sole vandal or a lonely serial killer.

Why is it usually so heartless? Alienation may explain this in part. If we feel ourselves separate from other people, it is obviously easier for us to hurt them than if we are attached to them. But why should we want to do this? The basic answer is that we have the propensity for anger, hatred, guilt and other destructive emotions. These, as we know, are contained in the cycle of ignorance/acquisitive yearning/hatred/ignorance/etc. that makes up the Three Poisons.

One possibility which I mention most tentatively is to do with the part of the brain which has been identified as our residual reptile brain. It lurks, so to speak, under layers of consciousness concerned with mammalian and specifically human behaviour. However, it has been held responsible for some of the more pointless and revoltingly brutal crimes. It is a hypothesis perhaps worth testing that in extreme cases the shocks which seem to lead to alienation open up easier access of this primitive organ to other regions of the brain.

But we live in times which appear to intensify this general negative potential. Much of the world has been to a greater (recently) or lesser extent in a ferment of change for considerably more than two generations. Thus large parts of the world are populated by people who have never been effectively adjusted to or integrated into society, and are becoming progressively less so.

A further personal experience may be useful to illustrate how alienation can occur.

My first professional task was as a research officer to an organisation that was working for British army soldiers who had been prisoners of war during World War II. Most of them were men who had been in captivity for five years and who, shortly after return home, had become very distressed. Some of them showed neurotic or psychosomatic symptoms but others, without being diagnostically pathological, could not adjust themselves to ordinary life. A much higher proportion of them than of the population at large, or of other ex-soldiers, quarrelled violently with their wives and other members of their families, left their jobs or hung around listlessly, slept badly and lost their appetites, fell out with neighbours or work mates, or were convicted of petty crimes. Moreover, we discovered that other men, some now very senior army officers, who had been prisoners in World War I, had suffered similarly and had gone on doing so for many years.

Psychiatric and psychological examinations were carried out on hundreds of these men. These concluded that they were not suffering from mental illness of any recognised sort, but from what today we might call a form of post-traumatic stress. We termed this *desocialisation*.

This hideous word implied an inability to conform to the (expected by oneself and others) norms of family and social feelings and behaviour. (I should say here that some of these norms, sexist or patriarchal, were not particularly desirable but that alienation from them was nevertheless wretchedly uncomfortable.)

Desocialisation, it appeared, had been caused by progressive removal from the accepted expectations, hope and fears of life as they had been known. The first step was into the army training camp where (as I know from experience) one was forcibly exposed to an entirely new ethos and way of life, one which aimed to transfer all interests and loyalties from home to military unit. Next came the even tighter integration into the battle group, with its very powerful emphasis on solidarity — on which in fact one's life might depend. Then, for the unfortunate, came devastating moment of capture.

Capture had two implications. In the first place, it tended to generate feelings of both shame and guilt for allowing oneself to be removed ignominiously from the battle. It also created the need for an even stronger integration with one's fellow captives; to survive emotionally and in some cases physically, an even more close-knit community must be created — one even further from and more alien to home. And finally, to all this would have to be added shame at one's impotence, anxiety about family members possibly being bombed at home, and the discomforts and indignities of captivity.

(My work was carried out in what were called Civil Resettlement Units, a title which well describes their task: to help the ex-prisoners of war to settle back happily into civilian life. This will be discussed later. Here I only want to describe a condition which may help the diagnostics of violence.)

Let me now add a further personal experience. As a young man rising twenty I was travelling in Lapland, a sort of rehearsal for life as an anthropologist (which in fact I did not become). After living for a few days with a group of Same travelling up into the hills to herd reindeer, I felt acutely uncomfortable and miserable. Everything the Lapps did rubbed me up the wrong way, and was virtually offensive. Then one morning, for no particular reason, the irritation suddenly cleared. I accepted their ways as being perfectly right for them and therefore, since I was staying with them, right for me too. I relaxed and was happy. Oddly enough, when I returned home I felt a similar dislocation from my own old life. In a few weeks this, too, had passed. But I experienced a valuable lesson about the ways in which we connect with society, and the ways in which the connections may weaken. In my case, however, there were no great traumata, no great emotional ties were broken.

Our century has seen innumerable situations after which this kind of alienation might be suffered: wars, drastic social shifts such as decolonisation and the fall of empires, economic failures and depressions, the experiences of forced migrations or concentration camps. Above all, perhaps, the swift, ever-rolling, unstoppable change in a society moving too fast for us to catch up with it. We tend, when it is associated with some identifiable incident or chain of incidents and when the symptoms are marked, to call it Post Traumatic Stress Disorder (PTSD).

All these factors can easily be the occasion for PTS, alienation and desocialisation — or perhaps it is more true to say that we feel there is now no worthwhile society to which we might relate?

Perhaps we are not so much alienated from society as from each other, from humanity? In general the rapid changes we have been discussing have opened up many breakdowns of comprehension and sympathy in society — especially between those who have profited from new opportunities for gain and those who have suffered from the same circumstances, and between different age groups such as parents and children: the twenty- and the fifty-year-olds see radically different realities and use different, mutually incomprehensible languages to describe them.

To sum up, the sickness around us and around our world, and probably touching all of our hearts in one way or another, is an expression of desperation and despair, loneliness and impotence.

Part of the despair comes from a dim awareness that we are separating ourselves from our own great potential for wisdom, compassion and courage; part of the desperation comes from being separated from a world which we see speeding past us, but which is going so fast that we can never jump onto it. We can drink, take drugs, descend into depression, or lash out — or alternatively kill ourselves in the sense of denying our potentiality for realising our true humanity.

In saying this, I am not simply speaking of the poor wherever they may be in Africa, the USA, Ireland or England. We are all in the same boat, the same ship of fools. In one way it is worse for the well-to-do of the West, they have further to fall and they know it; and the chattering classes have woven webs of illusion around their intellectual solutions, and lack the earthy common sense of the survivor. The poor of Africa and Asia have less to lose, are more inured to pain and have that keener sense of reality which they share with most survivors.

Unpeaceful relationships

Violence may also be defined in terms of unpeaceful relationships, that is to say relationships which cause suffering to one or both parties.

Each of us is involved in countless relationships, known and unknown. They stretch around the globe, a vast network having many different forms and emphases, knitting us together, weaving a subtle fabric through the psychic world. They are the channels of communication through which will flow all the messages of Mind to flood our hearts with images of peace or hatred. In their variety, healing and explaining, teaching, suffering and loving, they are like veins bearing precious blood to vivify the whole.

But we must keep the channels free. The blood of peaceful relationships must not coagulate in clots of hate or ignorance, to damage the free working of the emotional heart. We must explore the runnels of relationships, cleansing them of feelings that would block them, learning how the half-asleep machine that we can so easily become, responding to its hurts of fears, is trapped into illusions of separation, jealousy and envy, hatred and eventually violence.

Countless filaments connect in everyone. Thus in what we do and what encircles us we enact and duplicate the cosmos, the totality. We constitute a sort of hologram. We contain each other; in one sense each is each, helping — or in far too many cases hindering, even demolishing — one another.

It is both depressing and frightening to see how, for example in parts of former Yugoslavia where the population had been a mixture of Serb and Croat who had lived together in quiet harmony, the outbreak of hostilities led them to evict, to rape, to kill each other, and now to hate and fulminate against each other.

What had happened?

The soul wound

It is of course well known that most forms of neurotic disorder involve tendencies that create problems in human relationships — dependency, bad temper, suspicion, timidity, domination, too much or too little assertion, selfishness, subservience, shyness, etc. These are mostly thought of as arising out of some lack in the emotional nourishment in the childhood of those concerned: lack of love in particular, lack of wise and consistent care and understanding.

However, some therapists have noted that the failure of relationship has not arisen from any one or any combination of such qualities. These may or may not have been present, but the main reason for the breakdown seems to have been *a general inability to establish any relationship,* to achieve closeness with another individual.

Such an incapacity is referred to as a soul wound. The word soul is not used in any particular religious sense, but rather as the central or organising element in the mind, connected with what Jung would have termed the collective unconscious. The soul wound, according to Thomas Yeomans (see Bibliography), is inflicted when a child's parents or other carers do not welcome it into their lives as a whole human being (a soul, if you like), but as a bundle of potential capacities — physical, intellectual, moral, artistic, as a worthy heir to the family business, as someone who would be able to do what the parents never had a chance to do, as a preacher, as a great tennis player. And so on.

No doubt we nearly all suffer to some extent from the soul wound. I have only met a very few, the Dalai Lama was one, who seemed not to. But it seems possible that those born in certain uneasy periods would be more likely to suffer deeper wounds than others. Times of such deep stress and want that the attention of parents was preoccupied with the basics of keeping alive might be one — and these have been common throughout the century. Another might be times, such as the 1980s and the present, when material achievement is for many all-important. Thus the children of the ever-striving rich may suffer especially.

Indeed, simply to live in an age of rapid change might prevent the wound from natural healing. Moreover, when the change is accompanied by violent episodes it could precipitate a degree of unpeacefulness in relationships that leads to gross cruelty. Such I believe was the case in some of the extreme brutality in the Yugoslav conflict. We might term this Stress Aggravated Soul Wound.

If these hypotheses are even partially correct, the ultimate consequences could be very serious indeed. Unless social and psychological healing were systematically initiated in places where violence had been endemically rife, more and more women and men would be born in conditions conducive to deep soul wound. The effects on human society could be disastrous; even more so if the provisional theory regarding the reptilian brain were correct.

Why violence?

But finally the essential question: why should PTSD, alienation, anomie, desocialisation, soul wound (or whatever we may term the condition or aspects of it) and the associated negative emotions of despair, etc., lead to violence and cruelty? Obviously they do not do so in everyone, but given the 'right' circumstances, they can be easily evoked in many who had never previously expressed them. Bosnia abounds in evidence to this effect. Let us put together various factors which have previously been discussed.

I would refer first to the broad psychological / philosophical framework provided by the concept of the Three Poisons; this, it will be recalled, posits an element of hatred or dislike in virtually all of us. To this I believe we can legitimately add the natural, or 'animal', aggressive tendencies which may be evoked when we believe or are told that our vital interests are threatened. And in this connection the 'reptilian' brain may perhaps play a part. However, the concept of alienation and its synonyms or partial synonyms is more significant than the genetic ones, though they are not mutually exclusive. (I would stress, however, that those who act cruelly and violently are not necessarily more alienated than the alienated are cruel or violent.)

Alienation induces a sense of loneliness and separateness from the community and indeed from humanity. This, though it does not of itself generate violent acts, makes them seem remote from reality, less abhorrent. But it also induces a sense of impotence, for which we may try to compensate by violence facilitated by this remoteness; it is the only way, if bloody, of making a mark on the world. Also, of course, in our separation from society we are also separated from, and hence often deride and flout, its moralities. This contempt for the conventional 'good' has long been a streak in 'advanced' European thought. Sade always has a cultish following — such as Breton who felt that the 'purest surreal act' was to empty a pistol into the mob; and such, of course, as the Nazi intellectuals. But coupled with their 'avant garde' thought is the despairing self-hatred they share with the vandal who ruins his own home and environment, and with the guerrilla who kills without purpose, whose violence and torturing are a form of self abuse. When captured and restrained, these often commit suicide; the death of the body following almost naturally on that of the emotions.

Epidemiology of violence

It may now be possible to define slightly more precisely, but still tentatively, the various groups or circumstances, or combinations of these, in which alienation is more likely to occur. They would include:

1 Communities which had suffered the instability of war and / or rapid change; especially periods lasting more than approximately thirty years — that is, long enough for many adults never to have known *a sense of certainty*. (We have considered the cases of rapid change due to technological advances and decolonisation, sometimes the two coinciding.)

2 Groups which have been subjected to particular forms of stress (as were the former prisoners of war mentioned earlier in this chapter), homelessness (as among refugees), war, revolution, famine, long-term unemployment.

3 Oppressed minority groups. (It is of course natural that members of such groups should feel alienated from the oppressive majority, and feelings of despair and confusion at their fate can easily arise).

4 Communities which are separated from the wider society by an unbridgeable gap of poverty and other forms of deprivation.

5 Elements of society where the culture of acquisition (competitive materialism) is eroding the pattern of cooperative human relations on which emotional security depends more than it does on

prosperity. This is a recognised source of depression.

6 Communities where the traditional culture has been replaced by nonspecific universalised forms or practices having little social value; these might include a flood of videos (particularly videos of violence), inferior pop music, and the tastes of which MacDonalds and Hilton Hotels are symbols.

There is no suggestion that everyone who has been subjected to these types of conditions, or belongs to the groups just mentioned, will be emotionally driven into mindless violence. But in certain circumstances, those who are in any case psychologically damaged may be more susceptible to violent impulses; for example those who have:

(a) suffered a profound 'soul wound' (as already suggested).

(b) had particularly traumatic experiences.

(c) been exposed to extreme religious, racial and political views.

(d) addictions, particularly to alcohol and drugs.

(e) a dependency need for leaders whom they will obey without question.

(f) become inured to the experience of violence through example, or through constant exposure to violent videos or TV programmes.

(g) assimilated a highly macho and competitive culture.

(h) been brought up in a society with a war-like tradition (like that of the Pathans).

Many people whose vulnerability to violent impulses has been heightened in one or more of the above ways will not necessarily act violently. It is important to remember that even in the most adverse circumstances, far more people behave decently than badly. But in conditions of instability and conflict, actual or potential, it is unscrupulous leaders, fanatical, monomaniacal, and opportunistic warlords who come to the fore. They take control of or form groups with names taken from the initial letters of such words as freedom, patriotic, front, national, party, army, liberation, democratic, but which now have little to do with the ideals they should stand for.

These offer to confused, despairing and alienated followers the cold comfort of belonging to at least something which gives even the most dubious purpose to meaningless lives. On the orders of the leader, and eventually spontaneously, they may kill, burn, torture without guilt. And nothing is achieved save to feed the vainglory of a warlord or the lurid fantasies of a fanatic.

(I must stress that I am not here maligning the many women and men I know and respect, fighting honourably for a cause to which in fact I have not always personally subscribed).

Part II
Aspects of contemporary peacemaking

Introduction to Part II

Not many of our vicious contemporary wars end in what might be called a tidy fashion, with a cease fire, a peace conference, a settlement in which both sides are tolerably satisfied and finally a resumption of normal relations between the protagonists. The majority drag on until one exhausted side somehow manages to crush the other, which now longs only for the day when it is strong enough to fight again and wreak a harsh vengeance.

The same could be said of acts of anarchic violence by groups or individuals in the inner cities of the developed world. A violent and destructive young man (if caught, which few are), given a rough time by the police, sent to prison or some form of detention, is eventually released in a much worse state than when he first offended. He will soon commit another act of violence or cruelty.

In the case of large-scale conflicts the old methods have been almost entirely unsuccessful — intervention by the UN or the EU or the OAU, diplomacy including the arm-twisting approach of alternating threats and promises, intervention by private bodies or individuals, and old-fashioned gun boat diplomacy.

The reason for these failures lies in the nature of the conflict. The older and often successful methods were based on the assumption that the combatants were more or less rational; that they had definable objectives which might be achieved by some alternative means that they had not considered; and that they would be moved by what was surmised to be their self-interest.

But such assumptions are not valid in the tangle of phobias, cavorting egos, crazed convictions, vanity and greed that make up the psychic worlds of the mini-war. Big wars, fought by disciplined professional soldiers who recognise certain values and conventions, are very different. I am not suggesting that the time honoured approaches are useless — I have met many wise and able diplomats — but that they are not enough. Something else is needed if they are to be in a position to do their part of the job effectively.

So far as individuals are concerned, the situation is comparable. Two or three decades ago, the police in most large cities had a reasonably good idea of who comprised the criminal population. They could recognise the operational style of different burglars, knew their tastes and habits and only had to break down an alibi to get a conviction.

Now, however, the vandal, murderer or rapist might be anyone. Previously unknown characters suddenly become notorious because, like so many, they had a knife and, like too many, used it on scant provocation. The modern offender's violence is his secret weapon. Until he acts it out nobody know the dark side of his thoughts, his despair, his alienation from humanity. Because his crimes often appear motiveless, there are few clues, so he may never be caught. In addition, he is often drug-addicted, but whether it was the drug that stimulated the violence, or whether the latent violence demanded the drug, no one can tell. Careful detection, patrolling the street, restoration of good community relations, though obviously desirable, cannot of themselves dam the world's tide of crime; it floods over the forces of law and order as the waters flooded over Canute — but without teaching any salutary lesson!

Police forces deal with individual suspects and with gangs of crooks. Peacemaking bodies on the international or major internal war scale deal with the leaders of governments or guerrilla movements. In general they treat with people qualified to make decisions affecting peace or war.

But nearly all wars are civil wars (though some conflicts, for example in the North Caucasus of the former USSR, involve quasi or pseudo statelets). This may in itself imply the kind of breakdown and disorder which is responsible for the pointless violence we are addressing; there is, as it were, no really authoritative authority to deal with.

We don't really know what to do in these circumstances, and so tend to do the wrong thing. Like the USA blundering into Somalia to provide help to the suffering people, we end by killing those we seek to help. So it was also when the Indian army invaded Sri Lanka to protect the Tamils; things went wrong and it fought them instead — and lost. And so it was when the British army went into Northern Ireland to protect the Catholic population from Protestant violence and ended by fighting the Provisional IRA for twenty-five years.

What we need to address is not the impotent or corrupt or self-seeking rulers, but the confusion, the destitution, the misery and the injustices they create (if strong), or allow to occur (if weak), or simply inherit. We need to address both the social, economic, political and, above all, the psychological factors that create alienation, *coupled with* the other set of conditions that add cruelty and violence to the alienation.

Exactly the same is true of individual violence in places which are nominally at 'peace'.

In saying this I am making no vain promise to explain how it should be done. I can only pass on some ideas based on the experience of both my associates and myself which may suggest the beginnings of a fruitful approach to some of our problems.

I begin with some of the problems deriving from our own nature, because unless we are to some extent at peace inwardly we cannot effectively tackle the outer issues. I shall then move on to explore mediation as a peacemaking method. This, as will be seen, is based on psychological principles. It contrasts with some of the techniques being popularised today, ranging from bullying negotiation to verbal trickery, and which have little to do with the realities of human hatred and desperation.

The peacemakers

We have discussed some of the sources of violence in us, but we must not be too hard on ourselves. We also have superb powers for creating *peaceful* relationships. Indeed, there are far more of these than there are of unpeaceful ones, as we must all know if we look around ourselves. Kindly and warm-hearted women and men vastly out-number those who seem to be cold and cruel, but any increase in the latter makes itself horridly felt. Note that I say 'seem'; I am convinced it is an illusion that anyone is basically 'bad'. The mental and physical mechanism we are born with is perfect, as are those of animals. Things can go wrong afterwards, but I have never met anyone of whom I felt that his / her original nature could not to some extent at least be restored.

Sadly, what often happens is that in our disgust at what someone has done, we behave towards them in a manner that only strengthens the flaw. But it helps if we refrain from judgement, as do the Tibetan lamas, and simply think of wicked actions as 'unskilful' (that is, unskilful in the quest for enlightenment). Then, if we approach the criminal or vandal as though — no, not as though, *feeling that* — she or he is a decent human being, then that is what we will eventually find. This is not an unctuous pietism; I would ask anyone to test it.

But of course, all too obviously, things do go wrong. The potential of our nature is frequently blocked and few of us make full use of our latent powers of wisdom, strength and compassion. We have discussed the virtually universal vicious cycle of the Three Poisons which generally is the cause of this failure and the source of much unhappiness and destructive behaviour. Within the enormous range of this cycle there are two matters on which, in my experience, it is possible to focus effectively. These are the level of awareness, and the nature of the self or ego.

Awareness

There are many layers of awareness. At the bottom, which need hardly concern us, is minimal awareness brought about by injury, drugs or alcohol. At a much higher level is awareness which most of us experience only seldom: an instant clear understanding of everything around us, including ourselves. It is nothing to do with the intellect as we generally know it, thinking about things, working out solutions to problems, planning the week's activities, and so on. We experience something of it in the creative certainty which takes possession of us, for example, in composing a poem when we become aware of what must be written, or in moments of deep feeling, or in the sudden illumination of scientific discovery. In the latter case, the more mundane but trained and essential intellect may be brought to bear on the problem of devising experiments to prove to the world that the inspiration was correct. But few of us live constantly in this layer of consciousness, and so here is much that escapes us.

Most of us most of the time are at a slightly fluctuating level of awareness. We are carrying on with our lives fairly competently, doing what is needed adequately. But for much of the time we are in a sense asleep. We are not conscious of our own being, nor of our thoughts, nor our feelings, nor the sensations of our body. We are acting like a machine. And in one sense this is what we are. Our training and our life experience has programmed us so effectively that for most purposes we have no need to watch ourselves and to think about what we are doing.

Most of us, certainly I, can get up in the morning, wash and dress myself, exchange a few remarks with my family, and set out to work, catch a bus, etc., etc., all quite automatically. I am like an airman who has switched on the automatic pilot and gone to sleep. And asleep is what, in a sense, I am.

In one sense this is fine. I have programmes which enable me to do almost everything I have to without thought. Suppose I had to work out how to do up buttons or use a knife and fork every time I got dressed or had a meal. Life would be impossible.

However, what I am describing is life without a mind: while the machine is in charge the mind is absent. Hence the term 'absent minded'. And the absence of the mind can lead to great difficulties. I had a colleague, a world famous numismatist, who was equally well-known for his absent mindedness. He used to rely on his secretary to stick a note in his breast pocket telling him what he was going to be doing, when, and where. This left his mind entirely free to wander around his collection of coins. Every so often he would look at the note and obey its instructions to give a lecture, go to a meeting, or lunch with a colleague. One day his mind came back from thinking about the numismatic department of a particular museum to find his body on a plane. He felt in his pocket to find out where he was going and why. But the note had fallen out. There he was, flying he know not whither, for a completely unknown purpose.

The professor's predicament was, of course, comic rather than serious. But I chose the analogy of the automatic pilot on purpose. Not every exigency can be programmed for, either on the machine or in our memory. An unprogrammed emergency can cause a fatal crash. What we cannot be programmed for is dealing with those issues of human relationships or moral decision that demand the highest degree of sensitive awareness.

But awareness is not only of importance in avoiding disaster. The extend of our awareness is the extent of our appreciation and enjoyment of every aspect of life, and the extent to which we contribute to it through the greater realisation of our potential.

Being more aware of ourselves, feeling more acutely the reality of our being, is the first step to feeling — rather than just knowing intellectually because we have read it or been told it — that we are truly interconnected with others, indeed with all life. We then begin to perceive ourselves and our friends, indeed everyone we meet, much more as in reality they are: interacting elements in the great system of life. It is this precognition that enables us to play a significant part in peacemaking.

Ego, the false identity

I am asked the identity of my friend and answer: Joe Brown. If pressed further, I add that he is a teacher, aged forty, married with two children, who lives in London. And that's that.

But if I said that the name of that body / mind combination is Joe Brown which contains a number of sub-personalities, I would be more accurate. They all affect each other in various ways, but there is one who predominates when he wants to impress someone; one that emerges when he's at work; another when he's at home; another who is a frustrated artist; another who is a frightened little boy abused by his uncle; yet another surfaces when he's in love; one who has bizarre erotic urges; and so on. The standard Joe is a sort of average, but you should not be surprised if you encounter any of the fringe versions. They are equally real.

And everything is always in a state of flux. Nothing is permanent. Our sub-personalities alter, as do the situations which bring them to the front of the stage. If we try to fix them in some sort of stability, they merge or fade or slide away.

So what is Joe's true identity? It is the Mind, the Mind which governs the thinking apparatus of the brain and which links us all in the shared life of the planet. It is expressed through a combination of genetic and situational / educational potentials which make Joe different from his sister Jane, but not better or worse than her.

The different sub-personalities are not necessarily important in themselves. They are the imprints of experience on the potential and can indeed by used constructively. On the whole, however, they tend to mask Mind and to obscure its clarity.

In this way they contribute to that ignorance which is the driving force of the Three Poisons. In this way they also contribute to confusion and uncertainty about who we are.

As a result we try to fill the gap of ignorance by creating an identity which will satisfy us and hopefully others. For this purpose we make use of the various skills, experiences and attributes which we imagine (sometimes falsely) to be at the disposal of our different personalities. We cobble together a self-image which may in fact be very different from what our friends see.

The whole process is, of course, largely unconscious. It is a selection of whatever we feel to be good, successful, impressive about our achievements and our character. And pathetically this may lead to bragging and exhibitionism which those we want to impress find distasteful. Some of it emerges also at a conscious level when, for example, we are writing an application for a job, but the real false identity is much more subtle.

The false identity may be woven around something which is very fallible, such as sporting ability or personal appearance or business acumen. These things become the real me, the essence of our being. When we lose an important match, or our looks, or go bankrupt, it's much more than an upset or a worry. It's a threat to our very being which may lead to what is called an 'identity crisis'.

The false identity, the ego, the 'I', is something that gets between our true identity of Mind and the feelings and actions by which we may express it in peacemaking or other forms of compassionate action. We shall consider shortly and again later in the book what may be done to increase awareness and neutralise the false identity. At the moment I will only suggest that whenever we use the words 'I', 'me' or 'mine', we try to remember to ask ourselves: who is this I; does it really think or believe this or that; is it right to associate this whole being with such a statement or opinion?

Nonviolence

The issue of nonviolence is inextricably interwoven with those of awareness and identity. The quality of nonviolence is intrinsic to peacemakers.

Nonviolence, it need hardly be repeated, is not simply a matter of abstinence from physical or verbal violence, it is an attitude of mind, an emotional orientation towards loving care and concern. The fully nonviolent person does not have to restrain violent impulses; she or he does not feel them. Admittedly there are degrees of nonviolence. Some of us are more profoundly or consistently nonviolent than others, some do have outbursts which have escaped the restraint of awareness. And of course some, on the other hand, are extremely and constantly violent.

Nonviolence is a product of inner unity. Those who are most nonviolent are the least torn by divisive sub-personalities, by guilt at their ignorance of their true nature, or by the urges and yearnings of the Three Poisons.

For this reason they are very strong. Their potential for power and decisiveness is not vitiated because their energy is being drained away by negative emotions such as worry, self-pity or dislike. They can devote all their strength of mind and body (the two of course being intimately linked) to whatever needs to be done.

It is for this reason that Gandhi said that nonviolence was the greatest power on earth. And it is remarkable how much is achieved by those in whom it is most unmistakably manifested — the Mahatma himself, Martin Luther King, the Dalai Lama. But Gandhi also said that to be truly nonviolent was exceptionally difficult. If we feel unable to tackle difficult tasks nonviolently, it was better just to do the best we could when faced with a violent situation; to do nothing would simply compound the violence.

As I wrote the last few paragraphs I mentally winced at the constant repetition of the word 'nonviolence'. It gives a negative impression. It is like saying to a lover, 'I nonhate you'. Even the Hindi words *satyagraha*, soul force or truth, and *ahimsa*, harmlessness, at least to the Western mind are a trifle flaccid. I try to emphasise in my workshops that what I mean by nonviolence has nothing to do with nonaction. It is an attitude of mind, as I said, but an attitude focused on doing, on working vigorously and joyfully on some great task to the glory of creation.

Action

The implication of what we have been discussing in the last few pages is that before we can act fully effectively on matters of violence and related ills, we must try to do something about ourselves. But what? It seems so much easier to go out and to do something about another person or situation than to change our own habits of thought and action.

There are, of course, countless methods of thought and prayer, yoga and psychotherapy. The world's religions and psychological systems offer suggestions from the sublime to the absurd — and even the latter might be effective in some cases. Individuals have to make their own choices. I can only say that I believe it is important to make a serious choice, and then to stay with it.

I put my faith in a system of meditation which enables me to still the surface turbulence of my thoughts and feelings and thus to be in closer touch with what I believe to be more universal and more long-lasting. This is what I have referred to as Mind. From this I feel able to draw a measure of calmness and understanding which would not otherwise have been accessible to my normal thought processes. The sorts of analysis I have tried to make in much of this book, especially in this particular chapter, have helped and encouraged me in this respect. These are derived from contemporary humanistic psychology and from what is known as the 'perennial philosophy', the common ground of mystical experience garnered by the profound students of all faiths, particularly Buddhists of the Tibetan tradition.

If I did not believe (as a matter of experience rather than blind faith) in the nullity of the false identity or ego, and in the inter-being of all things and their impermanence, my life would have been much less happy and more confused than it has been. But I am also certain that my pondering and meditation on these and other matters would be useless if I did it solely for my own enjoyment and peace of mind. It is only worthwhile if its purpose is to increase my ability to serve others.

Soft mediation

My first attempt at peacemaking occurred more than forty-five years ago. I never thought of it as peacemaking, still less as mediation, a word which hardly anyone used until much later. However, on looking back, I see that it contained most of the basic elements of much that has preoccupied me since 1965. With one exception: the situation was, as I have said, not violent.

The work with former prisoners of war that I have already referred to was carried out as a member of the army towards the end of World War II, but my colleagues then were the women and men who were in the process of setting up the Tavistock Institute of Human Relations and my first regular paid job as a civilian was as a staff member of the Tavi, as we called it. The work of the Tavi was at the interface of the psychological and the social, particularly where there appeared to be disharmony. It was especially concerned with situations where there was unrest and dissatisfaction when there was apparently nothing wrong with living or working conditions. Some of my friends referred to their work on these problems as social psychiatry. A number of them were psychoanalytically trained and much influenced by the object-relations theory of Melanie Klein and the group work of W. R. Bion. In the same way that Klein identified the influence of the different 'objects' or sub-personalities within us, and Bion analysed the effects of these on the members of his small groups, so they also explored the role of such forces in a system of interaction within the school, factory or community. It was an exciting period; we felt we were on the edge of great discoveries.

Dartington Hall

I joined the Tavi staff to carry out a particular task. The Tavi had been approached by the trustees of Dartington Hall to do a study.

Dartington Hall was an estate in South Devon (it still is, but after nearly fifty years, it is so different that it is more accurate to speak in the past) which was established in the 1930s to explore ways of revitalising rural life in what was then a particularly run-down area.

Its founders were Leonard Elmhirst, an Englishman from a landowning family in Yorkshire, and his wife Dorothy, a very wealthy American. Leonard was particularly interested in agriculture and rural industry, and Dorothy in education and the arts. The physical core of the estate was the fourteenth-century hall and adjacent courtyard. The hall was superbly restored from near ruin and the setting was superb, with views into the Dart valley and the wonderful garden, one of Dorothy's interests. Around it were 1100 acres of farmland, and woods run by the estate's farm and forestry departments. There was an arts department which sponsored a number of activities and ran courses for practitioners of various arts; there were schools catering for children from kindergarten through secondary school; there was a large building firm; and from time to time experimental businesses (today very considerable) and rural industries. There was what might be thought of as a little village including a small general store and a club, equivalent to the village pub, in the vicinity of the hall. The majority of the estate workers (the teachers in the schools and workers in the various enterprises) lived in this neighbourhood. The trustees were Leonard and Dorothy and three or four others, including Leonard's brother. They met every few months. But Dorothy and Leonard, as both the founders and the only resident trustees, had a preponderant influence on trustee opinion and on the day to day policy of the estate (though it must be said that forestry and education had virtually complete autonomy except in the appointment of senior staff). Leonard, thought not directly involved in local government, was extremely interested in the neighbouring area, particularly the area south of the nearby town of Totnes known as the South Hams.

It was not made clear to me — possibly nobody had decided — what I was supposed to enquire into: to follow the Tavi pattern of analysing the estate community and in the process to try to deal with any strains which might arise from the pattern of relationships, mainly those with authority; or to study the South Hams in the attempt to discover social / psychological factors responsible for their agricultural, and indeed social backwardness? Or what? It was a rather vague assignment.

I moved down with my wife and two young daughters in the early summer. We were lodged in two rooms in the courtyard, and ate in the communal dining room. Subsequently we were moved to the top floor of a large house which we shared with others.

Like all visitors, we were enchanted by the beauty of the place and delighted to meet so many friendly and interesting people. I spent the first few weeks simply going around and talking to people of every sort connected with the estate — the teachers, artists, administrators, secretaries, technicians, maintenance staff, and of course Dorothy and Leonard and any other trustees who happened to be visiting.

I also travelled about in the South Hams by bicycle to the little villages tucked away between steep hills. This was hard going by pedal power.

Before much time had passed, looking back, I think about a month, I felt that the most important and definable job was to work with the estate. The reason for this was that I found, in spite of the great attractions of Dartington, there was also a great deal of anxiety and dissatisfaction. Working conditions were very good, the housing was excellent, and no one could complain that the trustees were unpleasant or demanding — on the contrary, they were remarkably concerned for the well-being of everyone involved with the estate, and there were many examples of their generosity and helpfulness.

Why, then, the underlying negative attitude? I say underlying, because it was not usually voiced on first meeting. It was only when I had got to know people a little better, had spent an evening drinking beer with them at the White Hart club, that they would open up.

The reason for their initial reluctance to talk was in fact one aspect of their negativity. They felt some shame at being unhappy with conditions which most people would have envied; they also felt guilty of ingratitude to the trustees who were doing such excellent things and who had provided them with such desirable jobs and homes; but they were also afraid that if these feelings became known, the trustees would not only feel hurt, but angry.

This fear touched the core of the situation: the trustees, kind and good-hearted people, also had supreme power within the confines of the estate. They could hire and fire; what satisfaction is there in home and employment, in good schooling for the children, in idyllic country, if all these things can be removed in a moment of pique or at the whim of the trustees? The Tavi psychoanalysts spoke of the child-parent relationship, of how we wish to please the parents both because we love them and because we feel the need to placate — and because we also hate them for having the power we must placate.

The psychic atmosphere was thick with rumours of which the great majority were entirely false. But here is a familiar vicious circle: because we are frightened, our imagination fabricates reasons for our fear and then these reasons intensify our anxiety and become very hard to eradicate. Which comes first? It is probably impossible to say; as we have already seen, things grow together in the same soil, affected by the same poison, and providing the conditions for each others' growth.

However, it is only fair to say that the trustees did do some things which, though justifiable in terms of their own aims, gave grounds for unrest. And the fact that people had no reason to complain, having accepted the conditions of service, did little to diminish their anger and unhappiness. People were hired for projects which for a variety of reasons were abandoned and the people were then dismissed and had to move from their houses which were all tied to employment on the estate. Or newcomers were immediately given estate accommodation ahead of people already working on the estate, but for whom there was either no or only inadequate estate housing.

Oddly enough, my own situation subsequently fuelled distrust and dissatisfaction. We were quite contented with our new home, but were surprised when childless relatives of one of the trustees were moved into an empty single house next to where we lived on the top floor of a large building. There you are, people said to us, that's a good example of how things are done.

There were other matters, largely to do with their status vis-à-vis the local government Rural District Council, which were a cause of complaint. They were not in a position to raise objections or to make suggestions. But housing was the main issue. Although most families were involved with teaching and really very safe, people who worked with one or other of the more experimental projects felt that the stability of their families was very precarious — especially in a post-war period when demand for houses exceeded availability. And their uncertainty was contagious. I came to feel that the question of accommodation was the hinge on which the morale of the whole estate was hung. I decided to concentrate on this.

The allocation of accommodation

For the trustees, too, housing was the main issue. When I tentatively raised the matter with them for the first time, they were sympathetic, but firm. This is something we have to control, they told me. We may need someone to play a crucial part in some activity and if we are unable to offer suitable accommodation, they just won't come. We can't put them off because someone else who is not essential to the work has had another baby and so wants to move to a larger house. And we can't allow people to stay on after their job has come to an end; we just don't have enough accommodation.

When I talked with members of the estate (those who worked there and their husbands or wives), they were understanding. We do see their point, they assured me. But what hurts us is that they don't trust us to be sensible. They are so nice, but so arbitrary; it makes us feel we can't discuss things with them. And that gives us a bad feeling.

Some went on to say that if the trustees would openly discuss the problems of house allocation with them, they would feel much happier. Others, however, said this might just make things worse. They would all have a cosy chat together, and then the trustees would simply go and do whatever they had wanted to do all along. Then people would feel that any consultation was just a sham to improve the trustee image of democracy without doing anything to justify it. This would be bad for everyone.

Issues in mediation

So I came up for the first time against two perennial issues: those of trust, and of the mirror image. Any serious quarrel is made more difficult to resolve because the protagonists neither believe what the others say, nor that they will behave honourably and decently. The mirror image is that each side sees in the other what the other perceives in it. In the case of Dartington Hall, the trustees saw the estate members as selfish and irresponsible; the estate members saw the trustees as being selfish in that they put their own interests first and irresponsible in that they did not care whom they hurt in serving those interests.

I must add, however, that in this case there was one very large difference from what is usual in cases of hard or violent mediation. These feelings were all tempered — but also confused — on both sides by genuine goodwill, liking and respect. But this conflict of feelings complicated the situation. It provided a leaven of affection and concern, but also guilt.

The first objective in most mediation is for mediators to gain the confidence of both sides. Without that there is little chance that they can be induced to have direct dealings with each other. They have to trust the mediators' assurances that they will not be tricked into a false position, or humiliated, or — in cases of hard mediation — kidnapped and assassinated.

However, even when they have faith in the goodwill and competence of the mediators, they may have misgivings which are difficult, indeed sometimes impossible, to overcome; their hatred is so virulent and their suspicion so deep-rooted that they cannot bring themselves to believe that any good could possibly come from a meeting with their sworn enemies.

All that the mediators can possibly do is to plod on with infinite patience, trying to reduce the tension, trying to change the perceptions each side has of the other. They must pin their hopes on that very impermanence which in other circumstances many of us dread: the alterations, slow or at times sudden, of mood; for a change of actors by death, rebellion, or retirement (which is uncommon); for some sort of external intervention.

If we scale down these bleak alternatives to the Dartington Hall level, the picture is, of course, much gentler. In fact, there is no problem about getting people together; they live in the same area and may meet each other frequently on the business of the estate, or simply walking around, when they would greet each other genially in passing. But not to talk about the hidden aspect of their relationship to each other; not about the latent power the one has over the other.

I realised that if the morale-damaging situation I had identified was to be remedied, there would have to be a genuine meeting of minds, a real exchange. Looking back to the late 1940s I realise that what I tried to do then (successfully) was similar to what my colleagues and I were trying to do (unsuccessfully) four decades later — to bring together representatives of a government with those of a guerrilla movement. In both cases the resistance to direct talks (as opposed to proxy contact via mediators) came from what appeared to be the weaker party: the guerrillas and the estate members. The government and the trustees both felt sufficiently secure to run the, to them, very slight risk of open debate.

The Estate Committee

It seemed to me that if a productive debate were to occur it must be within some sort of framework. It was not something that could be worked out solely by individuals, by individual estate members or by Leonard and Dorothy. A corporate agreement would be necessary rather than a friendly but essentially unofficial accord between non-representative men and women. But then, as I thought about the problem, I discovered that there was in fact a 'constitutional' body, the Estate Committee, which brought together what could be thought of as the management (in the shape of Dorothy who chaired its meetings) and representatives of the employees. It was as though members of the guerrilla band, disguised as ordinary citizens, debated with the government in a parliament of which a high ranking minister was Speaker. They would feel at a distinct disadvantage, but at the same time obliged to be on their best behaviour.

The Estate Committee was empowered to discuss anything, apart from details of work and projects, to do with the welfare of the members of the estate community. Hypothetically, it could have discussed housing, but this was too sensitive. To do so would be tantamount to the guerrillas having to discard their masks and reveal their true identity as rebels — and so be in peril of being taken off and shot. Instead, therefore, the committee's meetings were preoccupied with such anodyne topics as the estate Christmas party and a children's summer camp.

I attended several meetings of the committee. Some of the members I already knew as being well-balanced and good hearted, and I visited many of them for long discussions at their homes. At first they expressed considerable resistance to the idea of using the Estate Committee as a forum for airing the key topic. They feared they might become dangerously unpopular.

I had similar meetings with the trustees, individually and together as a group.

In meetings with the members, I paid particular attention to the questions of trust and responsibility. I explained that the trustees, while wishing to maintain a friendly and democratic community, did not trust the estate members to behave responsibly where trustee interests were concerned. This could mean that they behaved in a way that did not accord with the general economic well-being of the estate; and that this, in fact, would be detrimental in the long run to their own interests which they thought they were serving.

We considered a principle which long after I came to recognise as of great importance in earning trust. It was often not enough to come up with sensible and constructive proposals; they would be much more attractive if the proposers suggested a course of action which committed them to something they would *sooner not do*.

On a larger and more violent scale, this might entail proposing a cease fire, which had tactical disadvantages. The proposers would thereby emphasise that their hopes for what a settlement might bring were greater than their fears of possible detriment.

In the present case, the disadvantage for the estate members might be that instead of sitting through these bland and cosy meetings, they actually gave themselves quite a lot of work to do. We agreed that if they were to bring up the topic of house allocation, it was not enough simply to protest at the way it was being done. That would only raise hackles without achieving anything.

The best way to bring about any change in trustee policy would be to make a suggestion about how the allocation might be done in a way that would seem more just, and would also allay the fears felt by the trustees; this could be achieved by offering to take on responsibility for implementing at least part of the proposals.

Several weeks went by in discussion with both trustees and estate members, mainly with the latter. When it seemed that both sides were ready for a serious discussion, the question of housing and one or two other minor changes were put on the agenda of the next meeting. The trustees were fairly well convinced that the estate members would not abuse the power that they were asking to be entrusted to them; the estate members were fairly well convinced that the trustees would not take their actions amiss. Nevertheless, I think everyone, including myself, felt a certain trepidation as the day of the meeting approached.

But in fact the various motions were passed easily and with much good humour. The final stage of the process was a large meeting open to anyone involved with the estate. The proposed changes were explained, put to them, voted on, and enthusiastically (I hope my memory does not deceive me) accepted.

Conclusions

It is of course true that perhaps less was changed than unchanged. Certain inherent conflicts, of course, survived. For example, the trustees owned the houses and would continue to do so. They were the employers, who would still create jobs and bring them to an end. But the difficult and painful problems that would no doubt continue to emerge would be more open to straightforward discussion, or at least more so than they had been. The new method of house allocation in which the estate member played a prominent part was efficient and, if anything, more realistic than the previous somewhat haphazard approach of the trustees. There appeared to be a considerable improvement in morale.

What do we hope that such peacemaking methods will achieve? Not, I think, just a peace settlement: it might be unfair, or viciously punitive, like the Treaty of Versailles, or the people might still hate each other even if the leaders had reached an agreement. Not just justice, because it means different things to different people; each side considers it is fighting for justice so there is a different justice for winner and loser. I would say that what we hope for is *more peaceful relations,* because these are not violent and because violence is the prime cause of human ills, of suffering, desperation and alienation from each other and from life.

For this reason peacemaking is fundamentally a psychological activity although, depending on circumstances, effective economic, diplomatic, political, or other action may form a part of it. This example of peacemaking in what I term soft violence contains most of the ingredients of peacemaking in the hard violence of war. But there is one difference. In war the level of anger, hatred and despair is so much higher as to be essentially of a different kind from the calmer emotions of conflict at Dartington Hall.

Hard mediation

I should begin by making it clear that I am writing about mediation carried out unofficially, not by the representatives of governments, or of international or regional agencies, but by people acting independently (though this is difficult and often undesirable — the problems and difficulties tend to be excessive for a lonely operator), or working for churches, academic bodies, foundations, or non-governmental agencies (NGOs).

Advantages of non-official mediation

I write about non-official mediation (and indeed peacemaking in general of which mediation is only one facet) because it is what I know most about. However, my experience has brought me into sufficient contact with official mediation to make what I hope is a fair assessment of both good and bad points of each. But before mentioning these I should say that what is termed mediation by the UN or powerful nations is often nothing of the sort. It is better described as arm twisting: take this action which my government wants and you will be rewarded by a fat loan or a squadron of new fighter-bombers; don't take it, and aid will be cut and the planes will be given to your rivals. These deals will be carried out under a veneer of diplomacy, plus perhaps a mollifying pinch of genuine mediation if the negotiators are sufficiently sensitive. Nevertheless, this is not mediation in the ideal sense in which I conceive it: a process which, as well as contributing towards a political settlement, heals the wound of hatred and begins the process of transforming enmity into friendship.

An additional need for non-official mediation is that nearly all contemporary conflicts are intranational rather than international. The world is pock-marked with civil wars, small and large, in which a government is pitted against a guerrilla movement (or sometimes a number of groups are entwined in reciprocal slaughter for no clear motive). In many of these, where a state government is involved it is impossible for any external power to intervene without breaching national sovereignty.

It is for this reason that the Quakers became so deeply involved with the Nigerian civil war of 1967-70. One of the group, while on quite different business, happened to meet the then president of Niger, Hamani Diori. He was a member of a group of five African heads of state (chaired by Haile Selassie of Ethiopia) who had been appointed by the Organisation of African Unity to try to bring the conflict to an end. They were absolutely frustrated, Hamani Diori said, because the federal Nigerian government insisted that the war was an internal matter, an illegal revolt by one province (the Eastern Region, calling itself Biafra), and that for the group (or indeed any organisation) to have anything to do with the province would be an unfriendly infringement of Nigerian national sovereignty. The group believed that they could do nothing constructive without visiting Biafra. They felt they were not only being prevented from doing their proper work, but actually manipulated by the Nigerians for their own propaganda purposes. But, said Diori, the Quakers could go to Biafra and do what we cannot.

The same happened in relation to the Commonwealth. The secretary-general, Arnold Smith, a distinguished Canadian diplomat with whom I worked very closely later on in the war, tried desperately to go to Biafra, but the Nigerian foreign ministry was absolutely adamant.

A further advantage of unofficial mediation is that we are anonymous. Nobody knows us and so, on arrival, we do not face banks of cameras, or a cacophony of questions from journalists. There is no publicity to coarsen the sensitivity of our discussions. Although the confidentiality of private mediation has been blown from time to time, I and most of my associates have been very fortunate. Only once, during thirty years, has my work been publicised, and then only innocuously. In fact, turning the story around, I have found that journalists can be most extremely helpful and reliable. For example, in Sri Lanka we heard once that a particular journalist knew of our work and had been making enquiries about us. We immediately went to see him and said, 'We are aware that you know something of our work. We would like to tell you about it, but please treat it as confidential'. He gladly agreed to do this and in fact became a useful friend.

The non-official mediators have one final subtle advantage over official colleagues. The protagonists with whom they work will soon discover, even if they do not know already, if the mediators act correctly, that they are only motivated by concern for the suffering caused to both sides by the conflict, and by their determination to do everything they can to diminish it. They are not concerned about who wins or loses. They do not take sides, except against war and the waste and pain that it brings.

Once this is understood by the protagonists, non-official mediators are usually warmly received as friends and helpers. Official mediators, however much they may be liked and respected as individuals, are recognised as the agents of whomsoever employs them. If they are acting for a particular nation, it is recognised that in the last resort they will serve that nation's interests, even if they go against those of the country to which they are accredited; this inevitably introduces an element of reserve into their relations with the protagonists. A further advantage of the private position of these mediators is that they can be disavowed if for some reason they cause embarrassment, or even expelled from the country without causing a diplomatic furore: they are both useful and expendable.

Advantages of official mediation

Official mediators have some advantages over non-official ones. They have automatic entrée, such as an ambassador would have, to recognised authority. (The non-officials have to work for this, but in my experience they have always gained access to the highest decision makers, ministers or heads of state). They are in a position to make use of intelligence information, while the non-officials have to seek out their own sources such as NGOs, friends in various embassies, and journalists. This can be a trouble, but it also contributes to building up a network of friends; I myself have never experienced an inhibiting shortage of information.

A final advantage, trivial but pleasant, of officials is that they have much material assistance. Cars and planes and helicopters are laid on. Luxurious accommodation is provided free of charge (to them, at least). They have the use of sophisticated communication systems, whereas the non-officials may spend a whole morning in a chaotically crowded post office trying to send a cable or a fax. The officials pass without delay through immigration and customs, while the non-officials can face interminable hold-ups; I recall once, in India, bringing in a typewriter for a colleague. The documentation had been impeccably prepared and should have been accepted after a glance. But, oh no: the duty we were told we must pay was more than twice the price of the machine itself. In disbelief, we protested; the officials changed their tune about the amount to be paid, but were otherwise adamant. And so on, and so on. Then, after nearly two hours, they tired of the game. 'You may take the machine', they said with lordly detachment, 'There is nothing to pay'.

The difficulty of hard mediation

Once blood has been shed the problems of mediation at once

become intractable; even one death at the hands of the enemy trig-
gers a most profound archetypal response, as though the violence
that has brought it about was indeed a violation of the sacred. Deep
and irrational forces are stirred. This, I believe, accounts for the
horrid fascination of murder, both in real life as seen through the
media and through murder mystery stories. If Agatha Christie, for
example, had written about burglaries, her sales would surely have
been much smaller. I remember how deeply a friend of mine was
moved by the murder of a not very close relative; he was shattered
to an extent that he would not have been if she had died of an illness
or been killed in a car crash.

So the mediators are faced with some difficulties they would not
have encountered in soft, not physically violent, situations such as I
encountered at Dartington Hall. One of these concerns their own
position. Nobody at Dartington, or the few other places where I have
played a comparable role, worried much about my bona fides. I was
there, trying to do a useful job, and that was all that mattered.

However, if the quarrel has escalated into war, the position of
mediators is not only difficult but also precarious. When the atmosphere of violence has taken hold, there is a constant undercurrent of
desperation compounded of fear, anger, suspicion, guilt and resentment, and mediators may easily become its victims. I have
experienced this in several ways.

In the first place, even if the protagonists are eager to have the help
of mediators in extracting themselves from the trap of a violence in
which they are caught, they may feel dubious about the mediators
themselves. How can they be sure that they are actually up to the
job? Are they perhaps more partial to their enemies than to themselves? (It seldom occurs to them that partiality to *either* side is just
as dangerous to the cause of mediation in which each must have
equal faith in the mediators). Are they sufficiently experienced to
avoid misinterpretations or gaffes which could actually worsen the
situation? What is their motivation? This naturally applies most to
those who are not accredited representatives of a friendly government or an international agency; perhaps they are in it for personal
gain, cash or, even worse, publicity in the shape of articles or press
conferences in which secrets are revealed or false impressions given.

Desperation about the situation, centring on bitterness against the
enemy, may be transferred to the mediators. The psychology of this
is complicated. We, the mediators, are temporarily transformed into
proxy enemies. My colleague Walter and I have had this experience
on returning from the rebel 'Biafra' to talk with the federal Nigeria,

General Yakubu Gowon and his staff. Because we had met with the arch foe, Ojukwu, and presumably talked with him in the same way as we were talking to Gowon, some of his guilt rubbed off on us. Added to that, they just needed to let off steam and we were a good target for their frustrated rage at the rebellion; it would do no diplomatic harm, as it might have done if the US ambassador or the UK high commissioner had been involved — and we wouldn't take umbrage anyway. (I should explain that I tend to use instances from the Nigerian war, not only because it offered many telling examples of the principles of mediation but because it ended a quarter of a century ago and most of those involved are either dead or no longer politically active. Also because much has already been written about it, so I am telling no secrets).

In any case, these outbursts, if treated rightly, may be helpful. After a while, the loud-voiced tirade comes to an end. The anger has blown itself out, and the general and the others sit back, more relaxed and perhaps apologetic. They explain they have been under some strain and that what they have been saying is not an attack on us; we are just proxies for the real enemies. We have said nothing up to this point, apart from initial greetings. We have listened carefully, gauging the mood of our friends and feeling some sympathy for them. Now we tell them not to worry, that we understand how they feel.

This is the moment for a fruitful discussion. If at the outset we had raised any difficult questions, the undercurrent of angry emotion would have surfaced in a very negative fashion, based on feeling rather than good sense. Now, however, there is the chance of moving towards a wise and humane decision.

A third difficulty for mediators is that, however genuine the friendship of the protagonists may be for the mediators, there is always the lurking awareness in each that they, the mediators, have the same relationship with their enemies. In times of stress this will develop into a suspicion that the mediators actually favour those enemies.

I know of one case where such a situation almost led to a complete breach of what had been a very strong relationship. It was also in the Nigerian civil war. The mediators were working under the auspices of the Quakers, primarily the American Friends Service Committee. This work was considered to be so sensitive that it was not publicised at all, even in other branches of the AFSC. One of these was actually engaged in relief work in the same area. This branch published in the *New York Times* an appeal which showed a picture of a starving Biafran baby with the caption 'A peep-hole into hell'. The federal Nigerians were furious, accusing us of a partisan approach completely at variance with what we preached. They found it very hard to believe that the incident was not deliberate on our part; how could two bits of the same organisation each be so unaware of what the other was doing? At length we managed to persuade them, but there was a stain on our relationship, though eventually removed, which was painful to both sides for several months.

Misadventures of these sorts can only be avoided by good fortune, coupled with constant awareness and the consistent expression of goodwill. If we had failed in these respects, we would certainly have been told that our involvement was no longer acceptable.

This incident introduced a question I am often asked when it is known that I have been involved with people who are associated with abhorrent regimes, or who have themselves committed atrocities. My answer is that I am trying to assist in a process which will bring such evils to an end and that to do so may of necessity involve having some relationship with the people involved. This does not mean condoning what they may have done, but trying to create conditions in which they behave differently.

I also point out that I must have contact with the individuals who carry responsibility if we are to have any chance of affecting a total situation in which thousands or indeed millions of people on both sides, most of them having nothing whatsoever to do with the conflict, are suffering. To fail to do this because of scruples about the morality of those I have to talk with would be the most gross form of self-indulgence.

But there is a further, subtler and more sensitive point. In order to have an effective relationship with someone in this mediatory context, I must have a positive feeling for them. To the extent that I go to meet them with hidden reservations, concealing my revulsion with smooth diplomatic words, the meeting will be a failure; the enmity will in some way be felt and so reciprocated. I must work hard in myself to realise that this is another being whose humanity I share, whose actions might have been mine if I had endured the same circumstances, whom I have no right to judge, but whom my friendship might help to break the fetters of compulsion. And as the relationship becomes closer, so it becomes possible to express regret at or even censure of something that has been done. This then may be listened to attentively and without resentment. If, however, I had burst in at the beginning of the relationship and accused the person of torture or war crimes, that would have been our last meeting.

I must admit that there are people for whom I have not been able to feel much warmth. Only one, however, was the leading decision maker for his faction and he had powerful subordinates with whom I became intimate.

Finally I should mention a fourth hazard of mediation. Mediators may become very unpopular. I had once naively believed that everyone must love and respect them as workers for peace. Not so. In fact, sometimes the more effective they become, the more they are disliked. They are not usually unpopular with the leaders (though I know one who tried to assassinate a mediator, but for exceptionally twisted motives), because it is the leaders who sanction their work. However, there is normally a faction who do not want peace because a better deal might be gained after further fighting, or who at any rate want it differently. At least three people associated with our work have been assassinated during the last few years. I have never felt in particular danger in this respect except once in Africa, when the guerrilla group we were in touch with suddenly and for no apparent reason broke off contact and became unreachable. We wondered if they were debating what to do about us, but were not particularly worried as they included some good friends. After three days, however, contact was resumed with as little explanation as there had been when it was broken.

The atmosphere of violence

In the difficult circumstances of extreme violence and the distorted perceptions and exaggerated destructive and negative emotions that accompany it, what can mediation achieve? The efforts of a few individuals moving between angrily and intransigently embattled groups, whether nations, tribes, clans, guerrilla movements or bandit bands, can count for very little. Their efforts are in constant danger of being swamped by the tumultuous surge of paranoia, of a warlord's ambitions, of personal ambition, of the desperation of armies who no longer know why they are fighting.

However, as long as people say they need them, the non-official mediators will probably go on trying. If they can keep their own feelings more or less intact (it's impossible to do so completely) they feel it is worthwhile. Although genuine peace may evade them, there are always interim objectives which may be achieved. An exchange of wounded prisoners may be arranged, the passage of humanitarian aid may be facilitated, a cease fire with the eventual possibility of something more substantial may be brokered (twice in my experience, but it didn't last), a few individuals may be given hope and comfort. More important, perhaps, but intangible and hard to evaluate is the impact of trying, year after year, to emphasise the values of peace and truth, to remind leaders of the cost in human suffering of their policies, to give support and comfort whenever possible, to help in the search for less violent means of pursuing political goals: to try at least to do these things in circumstances which are not always easy or pleasant.

Rare miracles

And sometimes, in this welter of confusion, violence and sisyphean effort a miracle occurs. The end of the Nigerian civil war was in fact miraculous. During the academic year 1969-70 I was on a year's sabbatical leave from Harvard and living in London with my wife and young daughter. I had a visiting fellowship at the Richardson Institute (a peace research organisation named after the famous Lewis Fry Richardson (1881-1953) who made his name for his research on both war and weather. At that time I was writing a book called *Making Peace* but between chapters, so to speak, I would carry on the work in Nigeria.

One day I had a phone call from Arnold Smith at the Commonwealth Secretariat headquarters in Marlborough House in London. He had just had information that the civil war, which had been expected to last another few months, was rapidly drawing to a close. Everyone anticipated with dread an even worse massacre than those with which the war had begun two and a half years earlier. Smith asked me if I would go to Nigeria at once and, since I had a good understanding with the leadership on both sides, use my influence to prevent a blood bath.

I set off on the first plane. I had no idea what I could possibly do — stand like a traffic cop between two advancing armies trying to stop them? That scenario ended (in my imagination) with me being crushed and killed by both sides. But I was already too late. When I arrived the war was over.

Instead of the victorious federal army massacring their defeated opponents and going on to rape and pillage throughout the land, they treated them like brothers. Wounded Biafrans were driven to the nearest medical centre, they were fed, they were given money and their own rations by the Nigerian soldiers. The guns were silent. There were no rapes. A Biafran soldier told one of my friends, 'It was extraordinary; suddenly it was all over, nothing happened. We couldn't believe it'.

I couldn't believe it either. In the hotel where I was staying I met Eni Njoku, the Vice Chancellor of the university at Nsukka, whom I know very well and who was one of the Biafran leaders. He had been brought over to sign the peace treaty and I would have expected him to be kept in close confinement somewhere until he was tried for rebellion. But no. He was free to go anywhere and was happily meeting old friends from whom he had been separated for three years by the emergency. Like everybody else (except Ojukwu, who wasn't there anyway, having fled to the Ivory Coast) he was at once reinstated in his old post on full salary.

How had this happened? How was it that a conflict which had started with almost genocidally bitter bloodletting could end in such an atmosphere of reconciliation? The answer we were given by several people was one I would never had presumed to suggest. They said that the efforts which we, the Quakers, had made to tell each side the truth, so far as we knew it, about the motives of the other had gradually changed their perceptions of each other. One example will illustrate this.

On one visit to Biafra, were we taken to a market place where a single cluster bomb had killed 128 market women and their babies. When I returned to Lagos I told General Gowon about this tragic incident. He was saddened, but said that this was the sort of thing that happened in war: if the Biafrans (whom he referred to as rebels) came to understand this, they might give up the struggle. But I told him this was false reasoning: the Biafrans were saying that this proved their leaders' propaganda to the effect that Gowon's federal army was waging a genocidal war. They swore therefore to redouble their efforts; even if they could not win, it would be better to die fighting than to give up and wait passively to be slaughtered.

Gowon had previously complained of the bloodthirsty ferocity of the Biafran fighters, but when I told him this, he looked thoughtful and said, yes, he understood. Gowon was a kindly and generous man, and something of his spirit and ideals filtered down to his commanders in the field. But the milieu of violence dissipates realistic understanding of the other, so that it often has to be imparted by an impartial third party.

Failures

The commonest form of failure is when one protagonist or indeed both of them would like to see an end of the quarrel which has them by the throat — but not enough to make concessions that would be mutually acceptable. The mediators are unable to help them to modify their positions or to change their goals sufficiently to save the lives of the people or their towns and villages from destruction. I have several times noted that as the struggle continues, the protagonists become more obdurate. The atmosphere of violence tends in fact to harden and coarsen their values. Then the war will only end through the exhaustion and/or annihilation of at least one side. And it is at this stage that the original aggressors (if it is possible, which it often isn't, to apportion blame) ask questions bitter with disillusion. I well remember one of my Biafran friends, a distinguished historian who joined me subsequently at Harvard, saying, 'Why did we do it? We lost tens of thousands of our youth and a whole generation of our children. For what? For nothing'.

A second type of failure is, I believe, caused by psychological insensitivity. The mediators simply do not realise the problems they are facing. They do not realise that the protagonists, particularly the top leaders, must be handled with great skill and understanding. They are often people driven by obsessive or fanatical values and ambitions, as is suggested by their having reached this high position; if women, for whom it is even harder to rise to the apex of power in a normally male-dominated society, their aspirations may be even more extreme, and their reaction to opposition or frustration more furious. Strangely enough even experienced mediators and skilled psychologists sometimes fail to understand the psychological difficulties of mediation. They seem to be so certain of the power of logic that they fail to realise that feeling is even stronger. I was astonished when someone I respect greatly for both experience and ability told me sadly after the failure of one of the efforts to resolve an African conflict, 'We were most disappointed. We thought that we had got it all tied up; they accepted our arguments completely. But then emotion took over and everything unravelled'.

A third type of failure is, it seems to me, caused by misunderstanding the role of non-official mediators. They are not just official mediators without, so to speak, their uniforms, but essentially doing the same things (plus or minus a few items) as they are. No, their salient feature is that they are *not political mediators*. They have to know, of course, a great deal about the political situation, to talk political sense, and to make political arguments. But their authority is not political savoir faire: it is *psychological and above all moral*. This, at least is true of Quakers and others who have a church base, but it is also true of many others who are agnostics and atheists of all faiths, if I may put it like that. What matters and what gives them strength is their concern and compassion for the waste and human suffering brought about by violence. Sometimes I fear that we are so keen to demonstrate our political savvy that we forget that our main purpose is to effect a change of heart which will lead to a change of policy. No, if we have a strength which is different from that of the official mediator, it should be that *we begin with the change of heart.*

What does this mean in terms of our actual behaviour? Overtly, perhaps not very much. Covertly, that we cultivate our awareness of ourselves and of our role and act accordingly.

Contemporary hard mediation

Today's violent conflicts are so complex and anarchic that the conditions for practising mediation as I have described do not always exist. As in Bosnia, and as earlier in the Thirty Years War, there are often no clear-cut boundaries between the combatants. Sides change and aims alter in what is often a bloody free-for-all. As we shall see later we should not always see mediation as the standard response to conflict. Instead, we should seek to establish conditions in which mediation may be effectively practised in conjunction with other tools for transforming violent into peaceful relationships.

Mediation in Africa

To conclude, it may be helpful to mention briefly some traditions of African mediation, in both hard and soft contexts.

The first is that both the mediators and the parties in contention have a deep and unwavering respect for human life and the search for harmony. Mediators make no attempt to apportion blame, to say who is right and who wrong. They simply examine how the conflict may disrupt the harmony of the community and consider the responsibility of each side in restoring it.

Second, it is recognised that mediation takes time, and that mediators must approach their task with patient thoroughness.

The third principle is that the mediators are carefully chosen for their wisdom and impartiality, and for their appropriateness as mediators in a particular situation.

Their most valued skills are 'listening' and 'understanding' — in some African tongues these words are the same. When both sides have been heard and the problem is fully understood, the resolution is attempted.

The word 'settle' also means 'cut:': in this context it does not mean identifying the guilty, but identifying and cutting out the wrong that the problem gives rise to. Thereafter both parties join in a pact not to restart the quarrel.

Intervention – Interference

The history of the world is full of examples of peoples interfering with each other — and interfering is usually far too mild a word. The Europeans in particular have inflicted terrible damage on others by, for example, the slave trade, by destroying the high civilisations of what is now Latin America, by colonisation, by the Opium Wars in China, by gunboat diplomacy. And of course they have also done each other terrible harm, especially during the present century through the two most destructive wars in history.

I am referring, however, to a more modern phenomenon, a form of intervention which paradoxically is more or less altruistic, but which ends by being almost as destructive an interference as the depredations of the past. I am referring to activities which have arisen from the post-World War II activities of aid and of the intervention of UN forces in a number of trouble spots.

Let me say at once that I am not opposed to these. It is a most significant advance that the nations of the world have collectively agreed to collaborate in each others' development and to help to make and to preserve peace when peoples are threatened by violence. The work of the great international agencies such as the UN High Commissioner for Refugees (UNHCR) and the UN International Children's Fund (UNICEF), like that of national NGOs such as Save the Children, Oxfam and the International Committee of the Red Cross, is beyond praise. But there are also many failures, some of which have considerably set back the very causes they were purported to promote.

Aid and its perversions

There are various categories of aid in which the recipients lost more than they gained. Before outlining these, however, it is worth pausing to consider how to set about making decisions on development. Such decisions require deep and serious thought; no rules of thumb will do. First of all what really does development mean?

The conventional wisdom when I was first involved in the issue in the late 1940s and early 1950s, was influenced by what had apparently stimulated Western modernisation: industrialisation. But few people stopped to consider that this had taken place in a particular social and economic context; to plant a steel rolling mill (as was done in Ghana, Pakistan and no doubt other countries) in a remote rural area where there were few educated people and none with technical training and where moreover there was no particular need for the product, was a recipe for disaster. Nevertheless, it was to industrial development that vast amounts of aid were devoted.

There was a very general belief in the trickle down theory (and lamentably there still is in places). But again nobody took into account the political reality that a controlling elite is capable of blocking the runnels down which the profits might trickle to the poor who most needed them. When I was involved in development issues in Pakistan in the late 1950s, the great landlords, many of whom were also leading politicians, also headed the nascent growth of industry. No wonder the rich grew richer and the poor poorer No wonder that in Britain when Value Added Tax is applied to such items as domestic fuel, it is the poor who pay a higher proportion of their incomes than the rich — and suffer more from hypothermia to boot.

It was not until the 1960s that some economists, particularly Galbraith, pushed the idea that the missing factor in development planning was the human being who would implement it. A colleague of mine from Bangladesh told me, 'They consider a cow or a field or a tractor as a development project; but not the man [sic] who milks the cow, or tills the field, or drives the tractor'. Attention, but not enough, was then turned to such fields as education (in which I specialised), health, housing, social welfare and clean water supply. But even so, the approach was narrow and unimaginative. Health and education began to be more seriously taken into account, it is true, but not for the sake of nourishing the mental capacity of human beings as a worthwhile end in itself, leading to great personal and social enrichment; it was done to increase 'human capital' or 'human resources', because that would benefit the economy.

Some economists went so far as to invent a technique called Human Resource Development Planning. It worked like this: suppose the GNP of a particular country is $x billion. This, to support a population expected to expand by 15% in five years, should expand by the same amount. You then discover how many professionally and technically trained people there are to sustain GNP at its present rate and you multiply the number by (naturally) 15%. This ludicrous calculation was applied in all seriousness to educational planning in Nigeria: detailed figures were collected for such people as plumbers, journalists, lawyers, midwives, brain surgeons, accountants, plasterers, fashion designers etc., etc., etc.

It is easy to see now how much well-intentioned bad advice was given — I gave some myself. We were arrogantly pleased with what we thought of as superior knowledge, but woefully ignorant of local conditions or what the people most needed (though we thought we know what they *ought* to need!). We tended to assume mindlessly that what seemed to have worked at one stage in Europe or America must be best in Africa, Latin America or Asia.

We encouraged cash crop cultivation, which often had a disastrous effect on the local economy and on the local diet based on the varied traditionally grown crops and animals. One common protein deficiency disease got its name because babies suffering from it made the same grizzling cries, called *kwashiokor,* as babies whose mothers didn't have enough milk; but these were babies in the towns, fed on white bread and lacking the normally varied diet of bush and village. In addition, any prosperity gained from working on the coffee, tea, cocoa, or rubber plantations might be wiped out by fluctuations of the world market. However, since most of the tea and other estates were owned by foreign firms and run by their local staff and managers, it was in general only the poor who suffered.

I have not mentioned the problems of aid which is unilateral or which is dispensed by a consortium of nations, such as ply Sri Lanka with the resources to pursue its wars. These are the vultures of the donor flock. I recall at an early stage of my own development having a partial, but nevertheless rude enlightenment on this issue. One day I met a friend of mine who was director of the American aid agency in Karachi. He was in a towering rage because one of his proposals for aid to Pakistan had been turned down by the Senate. This was for irrigation works which would greatly improve the wheat growing capacity of the Punjab, which used to be called the Bread Basket of India (it is indeed still the most productive wheat growing area of the sub-continent). When I asked why this obviously (to me) important project had been turned down, he told me that there was a large wheat surplus in the US, for which Pakistan was designated as a profitable market for the very reason that its wheat growing capacity was insufficient. So what was the aid about, except to enrich the USA rather than Pakistan?

It is now very generally accepted without shame or equivocation that aid is expected to bring advantages to the donor, but the balance is often very uneven (this, I am glad to say, is not true of the altruistic Scandinavian countries and one or two others). In order to obtain what they feel to be necessary — all too often weapons — countries run up ruinous debts which cripple their development. Even when the debts are not excessive the conditions may be punitive: the recipient must sell his raw material cheaply and buy only the donor's highly priced manufactured goods; in addition he must grant him mineral, timber, and other rights and only employ his carriers. In many cases the donor thus extracts enormously more capital from the recipient than he has generously donated — even if the recipient is not already paying back a ruinous interest on a loan.

But it is not only the greed of individual donors that impoverishes the already poor. The economic stranglehold of the World Bank and the IMF, in order to sustain a view of global society based on the supremacy of money (and hence those who have it), imposes conditions which virtually ignore the need of the great majority of the people who do not contribute directly to the creation of wealth. The sort of economics which determines such policies is not a science, not even a gloomy one as Coleridge called it, but an elitist ideology.

One last evil perversion must be mentioned: the arms trade, which as several recent examples disgracefully show, may be allied to 'innocent' aid projects. It is a shocking fact that the five permanent members of the UN Security Council are also the largest arms merchants. They eagerly battened on to the tendency for newly independent nations to plan, before almost anything else, to build up their armed forces. And of course once a country has started down the military trail, neighbouring B and C and eventually all down to Z feel bound to do the same. It is tragic to consider what might have been done for the people of these lands if the money wasted on arms had been invested in their education and well-being.

Defining development

Earlier I asked the question: what does development mean? So far I have really been saying more about what it is *not*, at least according to my ideals. It is not simply the accumulation of national wealth, because that gives no indication of general well-being. It is not even a high score on a set of criteria which includes such things as life expectancy, calorific intake, general level of education, morbidity rates, and mean income. That is good, but it could be achieved in a militarised autocracy — which would also not be to my liking. (You will see that what is meant by development depends on our ideas of what is *good*!)

During the late 1960s, when as I have said I was coming to terms with such matters, I considered alternatives for development. What, I wondered — if I were a Black South African, a Guatemalan Inca, a Chicano in Harlem, or a Caribbean in Toxteth, Liverpool — would help me to feel at ease in the world; hopeful, not angry, not feeling pressured into desperate action but purposefully getting on with life? My needs could be subsumed under four words beginning with the letter 's'.

Sufficiency. This meant having enough of the things needed for me to develop my human potential to the full: health, food, housing, education and a friendly community.

Safety. This meant that I did not have to worry about the risk of violence from war, or crime, or from a corrupt or politicised police force. In other places, I would add death squads, interrogation and torture, gang violence. (Even safety from natural disaster might be added, since more often than not there is a human contribution of inefficiency, poor judgement, or neglect. In addition, at least nine of the great famines of recent years, for which billions have been disbursed in aid, have been directly caused or closely associated with war.)

Satisfaction. This meant that I could enjoy the safety and sufficiency in an ambience of flowing culture.

Stimulus. This meant that there was the possibility and encouragement to move on — to obtain further education and rise in a profession or craft, to participate more actively in cultural activities, to move to a different home or environment.

This may sound idealistic, but in fact it is what I have enjoyed for most of my life as have, I suspect, most of the people who read these lines. These conditions are obtainable (except sadly for the danger of war) in most countries except the poorest. Indeed, in some idyllic communities they existed until brutally interfered with; such were the Chakma of the Chittagong Hill Tracts whose destruction I mourn. What is needed is not so much cash (and much could be saved by disarming), but the political will of the country involved and the friendly collaboration of the rest of the world in not exploiting it. This may, of course, be asking too much. However, simply to view development from this perspective and not just as the creation of wealth, would be a long step in the right direction.

Finally, you may have wondered why we should discuss aid in a book about violence. The reason is that much violence, local or widespread, is related to resources, especially water resources, which of course can be affected — one way or another — by aid. Aid, effective or ineffective, is a part of the pattern of events influencing relations between or within countries. This obviously applies particularly to military aid, which not only reflects the donor's relationship to the recipient, but the donor's general international philosophy and relationship with other nations. The British say, for example, that they will only provide military aid in the form of arms sales to 'friendly' nations. But what are these? Not long ago they were any country that hated the USSR, and this included many of the most corrupt and brutal tyrannies. But who now are the friends and who are the enemies? The foreign ministries of the world make their arcane calculus; on that basis they favour A rather than B. Those who work for peace must be aware that such decisions may be made on the flimsiest ground of personal obsession.

The interference of military intervention

As I write, it is to be hoped that the interference of the British army in Northern Ireland will, after twenty five years, soon be coming to an end. It began, of course, hundreds of years ago when the English occupied Ireland. Since then there had been periodical 'troubles' as they were termed; if they had been in Africa they would have been called liberation struggles. But the latest round began, after a lull of some decades, in 1969.

The occasion was that there had been a series of civil rights marches on behalf of the Catholic population of Northern Ireland (still under British control after the establishment of the Republic of Ireland in the South). These were opposed with such extreme violence by the majority Protestant population of the North that the army was sent in to protect the Catholics. But many of the Catholics felt that the presence of the army on the streets had even more sinister long-term implications than the Protestant opposition.

The Irish Republican Army (IRA), which had been formed to fight for the country's liberation from English control, still existed but was more concerned with domestic Marxist politics and did not want to get embroiled in what was felt to be a temporary episode. Some of their members, however, felt differently. They split from the official IRA, calling themselves the Provisional IRA or the Provos, and after a number of episodes the campaign began which has lasted a quarter of a century.

The troops are still there, but in deference to the cease fire, which we hope will be permanent, wear berets rather than helmets when on patrol.

I spent a great deal of time in Northern Ireland during a period of five years when the troubles were at their noisiest — countless bombs exploded and rifle fire was common at nights — and got to know and like many of the leading figures in all the main groups involved. But I never got over the strangeness of landing at Belfast and finding myself in what felt like a war zone, but was supposed to be my own country.

I learned much about war and peace, violence and cruelty, courage and devotion, in Northern Ireland, and have written about this in earlier parts of this book. But I also learned the terrible dangers of military intervention. Even when it is undertaken with the most impeccable motives and implemented with the utmost restraint, the mere presence of a body of men armed and trained to kill evokes turbulent feelings that, in their turn, provoke explosive situations. Such was the fatal Bloody Sunday in Derry, in which the paratroopers shot and killed thirteen harmless protesters; this generated an emotional impetus which has survived for years.

I have already mentioned the extraordinary episode of the Indian Army intervention in the war between the government and the Tamil separatists, the Liberation Tamil Tigers of Eelam (LTTE). What the Indians had really expected to be able to do has never been clear — at least not to me. But they ended up fighting the LTTE (who were being given undercover support by the government) rather than the Sri Lankan army. They landed an army of over 50,000 troops — which was driven out by a force of perhaps 6,000 Tamils — having lost 1200 men, which was twice the Tamil casualties. This ludicrous adventure led quite probably, though it has never been officially proved, to the assassination of Indian Prime Minister Rajiv Gandhi by the LTTE.

Rather more recently the altruistic US attempt to take humanitarian aid to war-torn Somalia led to reciprocal killings and bombing raids by US war planes.

And now at the time of writing we have the ineluctable imbroglio of Bosnia. The correspondence columns of the press are filled daily with condemnations of the vacillation, incompetence and treachery of Vance-Owen-Stoltenberg, the UN, the European Union, NATO, and anyone else who has had the temerity to intervene in the sad affair. Undoubtedly mistakes have been made, but it is equally certain that nobody has produced a generally acceptable solution to the intractable problems. The UN, the EU and the rest have been accused of weakness, and certainly some countries were feeble or dilatory in their reactions. However, most people were aware that an aggressive intervention, such as the UN undertook in Korea, would risk engulfing the whole of Eastern Europe in war.

The compromise of sending troops, not as a fighting force but as protection for those delivering humanitarian aid, might have seemed reasonable, but now both aid and troops are in jeopardy. I believed, before the military arrived, that the aid could have been more easily and safely distributed without a military presence, seen as ambiguous by many and not quite impeccably neutral because sent by the UN which had imposed sanctions on Serbia. I spent some time considering the idea of a civilian corps to reinforce the UNHCR and other relief distributing agencies. It should include people, including some trained in mine clearance and in repair of roads and bridges, to reinforce the UNHCR and other relief distributing agencies. But it was too late then; now, however, with the possibly impending withdrawal of the UN Protection Force (UNPROFOR), it may be time to reconsider implementing this idea.

It has to be admitted that no one has any idea what to do about the situation. This seems to include one of the apparently chief characters in the whole chaotic embroilment, Serbia's President Slobodan Milosevic. The areas involved are hardly normal polities. Croatia; Serb-occupied Croatia — the self-styled Republic of Serbian Krajina; Serbia itself, which with Montenegro constitutes the rump of the former Yugoslavia; the also self-styled Bosnian Serb Republic; Kosovo, a province nominally semi-independent in danger of being sucked into the conflict; Bosnia itself; possibly some semi-separate entity of Bosnian Croats... these are either not recognised internationally or are very new and untried UN members, whose recognition was probably premature.

Such a ramshackle gallimaufry is a rich seed bed for the sort of anarchic violence we are discussing. Renegade Muslims join the Serb forces, local warlords spring up like mushrooms, violence and brutality are honoured. Even the recognised leaders, whose pictures appear in the press hobnobbing with Lord Owen or Foreign Minister Kosirev, hardly set an inspiring example, while the arch-warlord Karadzic, for all his poetry and folk songs, gives an impression both absurd and ominous.

In this fragmented and frenziedly disordered setting there appear to be no rules, no guidelines except the certainty of contradictions and the expectation that no promises are kept. The conventional practices of international relations and diplomacy simply do not work in circumstances so bereft of precedents.

It is up to us to break all the moulds of custom in trying to find *a new way* to deal with violence. But this is not easy. I have an uncomfortable feeling that we seek solutions in the same realm in which the problem originated. I am not suggesting that Britain and America are much like the Balkans. But some of our basic values are: our materialism, our belief in solving problems by violence, our racial or ethnic prejudices.

We must look for another way, not to intervene, but to be involved.

Nipping the buds of violence

Bringing conflict to an end: the limits of conventional means

Mediation is a valuable tool for peacemakers, but only at times of stalemate, or when both sides want an end to the quarrel so much that they are prepared to make a compromising bargain. And, as we have seen, most wars end militarily rather than diplomatically. It is obviously desirable from every possible point of view to prevent them from ever reaching the point where the tinder of violence ignites.

But such preventive efforts are peculiarly difficult. Resentful individuals are not easily calmed. They long, in the telling phrase, to 'have it out'. But when it comes out, it does so explosively and people's feelings, if not their bodies, are likely to be hurt.

On the larger scale, the wise use of international bodies and the cautionary words of respected diplomatics can be most helpful. But governments, at least in my limited experience, are loath to admit to the existence of problems serious enough to need some sort of intervention until too late; they feel it would be an expression of weakness, or are too busy with something else (such as an election), or hope it will just go away.

Alternative means of ending violence

Some years after World War II, when peace once more had become a serious issue, academics and others began to be concerned that the existing international machinery for ensuring peace did not sufficiently ensure it. Preeminent among these was John Burton, whose creative thinking has enlightened the field of conflict resolution and prevention (which Burton interprets in a manner he has named *provention*) for nearly thirty years. The methods he initiated, and which has been skilfully carried forward by such scholar/activists as Chris Mitchell, are based on analyses of conflict situations by social scientists. These are shared with the protagonists whose insight into the issues at stake may well be changed as a result.

Nonviolence training

A different approach was pioneered by the imaginative and forceful work of Jean (now deceased) and Hildegard Goss-Mayr. These two people evolved a system of seminars designed to help the participants to oppose *without violence* injustice and oppression. These seminars, given all over the world, were on the same pattern, although obviously the specifics of the various ills considered were different and required different details of treatment.

They start with a study of the principles of nonviolence. (If it is appropriate for me to give my own definition, I would say it means doing without harming anyone — including oneself by anger or hatred — what is usually thought of as only possible by violence). They use the authority of the Gospels (with lip-service to other spiritual sources) to justify this approach. However, although I do not myself qualify as a Christian, this seems to me perfectly reasonable. The teachings of Jesus, the Buddha, Shankara', Ibn 'Arabi, Mahatma Gandhi, Archbishops Desmond Tutu and Helder Camara, the Dalai Lama, Tolstoy, Meister Eckhart and countless others of all ages and faiths coincide on this point.

This is followed by a discussion of the methods and strategies of active nonviolence: preparation of groups, analysis dialogue, negotiation, mediation, forms of non-cooperation, civil disobedience, direct action, along with spiritually directed action such as fasting.

These are applied to an issue brought forward by seminar participants. This is followed by role play, in my experience a most powerful method, and evaluation.

Another early approach was that of Herbert Kelman of Harvard University who instituted the series of what were termed Problem Solving Seminars, combining Israelis and Palestinians in the common effort to understand, and so perhaps to modify, each others' points of view. It may well be that these contributed to the change in the climate of opinion in Israel that has led to the tentative moves towards peace.

In South Africa, too, it cannot be doubted that the giant shift in public understanding that made possible the abandonment of Apartheid was largely brought about by the Dutch Reformed Church. This was a complete reversal of former DRC attitudes which provoked a placard I had seen outside a church in Johannesburg: Those Whom God Hath Set Asunder Let No Man Put Together. It had been brought about by twenty years of debate and controversy, though I do not know whether there were formal attempts to bring together those of different persuasions. This did, however happen at

Cape Town University's Centre for Intergroup Studies, and no doubt at many other places.

In the last few years, however, there has been a remarkable growth in the number of organisations being launched and seminars (usually termed workshops) being set up for what can broadly be called peace work. The main emphases are mediation, providing various kinds of help in times of crisis, and forestalling the outbreak of conflict. Among hundreds of individuals, friends of mine have been working in several parts of ex-Yugoslavia; several parts of the former USSR including Moldova, Ukraine, Azerbaijan, Armenia and several North Caucasus areas; Liberia; Rwanda and Burundi; Romania; the Horn of Africa; Guatemala; South Africa; Haiti; the rebel areas of Burma; Sri Lanka; and Lebanon. I justify this tedious and only partial list by the need to show the wide spread of a new movement. There are of course many other people working in these and many other areas on a great variety of humanitarian and other useful tasks; I mention only those who are running workshops.

The emphasis of most of them is to *train*. It is to prepare people to play a useful part in resolving conflict, to help those suffering oppression to resist or those threatened by violence and chaos to survive, to protect those in danger of assassination, to care where possible for the traumatised and the other victims of war. And in some cases the task is to give further training to those who are already trainers (though the distinction does not seem to me to be very clear; I suspect that training for trainers mainly means a sharing among experienced people).

But what is important or shared is by no means homogeneous. Much depends on the background of the individual 'trainer'. Some may come with a background in counselling or therapy, or social science, or teaching (almost anything), or social work, or administration. Their particular understanding of society, of conflict and of human nature will to a considerable extent determine the nature of what they have to impart or to share.

Many trainers will, however, say that their workshops have the basic function of helping participants to appreciate and to make use of their full potential for wisdom, courage and compassion. This will probably often include coming to understand the point of view of a potential opponent or someone of another culture.

To conclude this outline, I should say that there are important new developments being made to internationalise training and to establish joint efforts between groups from different countries. One such alliance has already organised combined Swedish/South African projects.

Case studies of training

I can best describe the purpose of such training by quoting from a letter to me by Diana Francis, one of the most wise, honest and experienced people in the field, about workshops she had facilitated in Belgrade. Belgrade is, of course, the capital of Serbia, a country widely held to have been responsible both for the initial onslaught on Croatia (of which it now occupies almost a third) and subsequently for the war in Bosnia. There are a small number of people who remain dedicated to the ideas of peace and are struggling to express these as best they can, often at the cost of painful insult and unpopularity and, in some cases, danger.

> I'm not sure that I knew, to begin with, why we were going, except that we were responding to a request for help (described as training) from people who clearly deserved and needed it. I remember my — our — [she was accompanied by a friend] diffidence, our questioning of the likelihood of our having anything adequate to offer. At once level I still find it surprising that we apparently did; but I also feel our visits have helped. Our process each time was to spend the first phase of the visit reviewing with the group their current situation and wants for our time with them, bringing together an agenda for the available days — an agenda constantly open to adjustment according to emerging needs.
>
> What we have been able to offer has been, by our coming and our listening, recognition both of the importance and courage of the work being done by the group and the need of those involved for solidarity and support. We have been able to share something of the emotions, try to understand the pressure and exhaustion and offer encouragement and affirmation. This has in turn enabled members of the group to acknowledge and express their own feelings of pain and weakness, but also to celebrate their own achievements and potential together.
>
> We have, in addition provided facilitation for the group as it sought to *become* a group, developing a common understanding of its purposes and deepening the relationship between its members — as well as working through conflicts and tensions. We have provided a framework for evaluation and planning, and the initial sharing of concepts and skills, which could be called 'training', was clearly of importance to the group at the outset and provided a basis for continuing self-development and external training and peacemaking work done by its members.
>
> One other thing: the love and laughter and eating and playing which have characterised our times in Belgrade indicate the refreshment which has come to us all through this exchange — an exchange it certainly has been. I cannot begin to estimate the plea-

sure and learning that I have gained. But for our friends in
Belgrade, this contact with the outside world has been a lifeline."

The following extract from the report on the first Belgrade
seminar will show the more general principles that were put into
practice.

> ... We had been asked to do training for trainers, so felt that to
> spend the first day on group process and facilitation skills could not
> be far off the mark. We also used the first day to clarify wants for
> the rest of the week, and what emerged is as follows:
>
> Day 1. Introduction; thinking about conflict and training needs;
> agenda proposal and agreement for the rest of the week; thinking
> about group dynamics and facilitation tasks; role play.
>
> Day 2. Basic skills; listening and responding skills; respect and
> assertiveness; prejudice awareness; responding to strong emotions;
> conflict mapping; needs and fears analysis.
>
> Day 3. Helps and hindrances in conflict; problem solving model;
> stages in conflict and corresponding emotions; role plays; strategies
> for empowerment of oppressed groups, tested on examples; more
> role plays and feedback.
>
> Day 4. Mediation: function, needs, stages; role plays and feedback
> on visit to both parties and opening stages of face to face meeting.
>
> Day 5. Mediation continued; breaking impasses and building agree-
> ment. Role plays and feedback. The same scenario played as
> negotiation; discussion of differences. Exercise to experience being
> the object of prejudice. Thinking about he needs of 'group mainte-
> nance'.
>
> "Day 6. Agenda building exercise for potential facilitators and
> trainers. Evaluation: learnings and plans for the future. Goodbyes.
>
> "We evaluated each day as it ended and felt clear that the time was
> useful to the participants [most of whom were psychologists – A.
> C.] ... they have made arrangements to meet with a view to
> forming a group to work on conflict resolution training and the
> provision of a mediation service."

Another trainer is Rosaritha Jarman, who is a teacher and counsellor. She has lived and worked with groups in Moscow, but recently
she has been working with groups in the troubled area of conflicted
statelets in the North Caucasus region. The cultural and psychological context of her work is very different from that of Diana. I was in
Belgrade at about the same time as Diana, meeting the same sort of
people. I found them easy and delightful to get on with. There is no
doubt some cultural difference between Serbs and English, but our
common concern with and interest in peace issues seemed to override

them. I have not been in the North Caucasus, but from what Rosaritha says, the cultural and religious differences (many of the groups are Muslim) coupled with the experience of communism — including, for some, deportation and eventual return to find their homes and lands occupied — have created special problems.

The settings for her various workshops have not been homogeneous, so she has no standard model but "finds that there are nevertheless certain key elements that I try to use as guidelines. The first centres around affirmation, the second around listening skills and communication, the third looks at conflicts and what skills are required for resolving these."

The workshops begin, as do Diana's, with introductions and expression of expectation.

> I want people to know that they have a right to have needs and expectations and share responsibility that these get met... In traditional Russian education people did not have any rights to express their own needs or contribute to their own experience. I see this as a vital step towards people taking charge of their own lives rather than letting things be ordained from outside.

In working on Affirmation (especially in workshops with psychologists, a number of whom attended her sessions, as those of Diana, she may stress the elements considered by Carl Rogers as essential ingredients in counselling: 'unconditional regard' or acceptance of the other, 'empathy', and 'congruence'.

She finds

> exploring these three concepts very valuable both in listening to the other and in resolving conflicts and also in the way the students get in touch with their sense of self...
>
> After a simple exercise around such concepts as 'I have a right to be who I am', and 'I have a right to make mistakes and to learn from them', people shared that they did not believe that they had such rights... People felt they were violating childhood messages received from teacher or parent which said to them 'You have to be what I want you to be. Only I (teacher, parent) know who you really are'...
>
> People often work out in outer conflicts what are basically conflicts within themselves. Personal fears and anger can give rise to violent action. Affirmation, knowing and accepting ourselves and being in touch with our potential are steps towards conflict resolution.
>
> *Skills — listening and communication.* We focus on listening exercises and try to be where the other person is. Not to give advice, not to be judgemental but to fully accept the person where s/he is now.

In communication exercises "we look at 'I' statements, i.e. taking responsibility for or taking charge of our feelings and the effect that blaming language or 'you' statements has." With psychologists more professional concepts, such as those of Gestalt, may be used.

> *Cooperation — conflict resolution.* We start by sharing our under-
> standing of conflict. We find that it is part of life, that we need
> skills to change the danger into an opportunity. We look at active
> nonviolence and peace building... Much of this is through role
> play.

There is considerable variation in the focus of conflict resolution in Rosaritha's workshops, including neighbourhood mediation, the organisation of democratic meetings, and — in a situation of acute and violent conflict between groups — attempts to raise awareness among children of the two groups about each others' feelings. I found it interesting that, in the same social contexts but among adults, the group that clung most intransigently to their prejudices were the psychologists.

Another friend, John McConnell, has had a different sort of experience, since he has lived in the area where he was working, Sri Lanka and South East Asia, not simply visiting for a week tor two to give a workshop. As will be seen, this enabled him to deal very broadly with a variety of issues. He describes his work as follows:

> We wanted to make the different communities understand each
> other better, help them develop tools of peace-making which would
> help them resolve a conflict. More basically we wanted to help
> them see that of God in each other. That is, we wanted to help
> transform defensive hostility into a spirit of generosity and experi-
> mentation with peace. Accepting that the war was likely to go on
> for some time, we wanted to counter some of the suffering and
> psychological desolation it inevitably caused.
> We had many private meetings in our own home and elsewhere,
> and discussed the situation in depth. The confidentiality of these
> meetings allowed them to open up more than they would in a
> forum that was in any way public, and some honest and profound
> discussions ensued. In retrospect this, which we did as a matter of
> course and did not think of as a programme, was one of our
> strengths. My only regret about this is that we could not meet more
> folk this way.
> We ran workshops in peace-making skills with a wide variety of
> people — brickmakers, teachers, doctors, journalists and adminis-
> trators — and worked with them on handling the kinds of conflicts
> they faced. This was useful too, in that the workshops got people

thinking about new approaches to old problems. This was demonstrated by the large number of times the participants consulted us on particular problems relevant to their own situation. Though we tried not to be arrogant about peace-making, it must have come over that way to a lot of people. In retrospect, we should have done more research into the philosophical and cultural traditions of each side, looking for resources. Some of the studies I have carried out since would have been of enormous help.'

John goes on to say that there were other strands to the work: this concerned some of the practical problems of health, rehabilitation, and counselling for victims of highly traumatic experiences. Support was given to peace groups helping them to think through the difficult task of witnessing for peace in a difficult environment. Some people in danger of assassination were helped to leave the area.

The value of training

When I began to be interested in peacemaking through mediation, I was surprised and a little distressed that most peace movement people despised this as pacification, which worked for peace at the expense of justice. Although the majority were gentle and nonviolent, most of them believed that peacemaking was essentially a struggle against the oppressive power of governments (especially one's own) and their henchmen in the form of arms manufacturers, intelligence agencies, and the military. I believe in protest and defiance: official malice or *stupidity* should be assailed by protest and demonstration. But I could not accept that bad policies were necessarily made by bad men who should be hated and despised. Also, having been a soldier during World War II, I knew that soldiers are not all ogres, even though they have been trained to kill.

I tried, more or less in vain, to show that trying to end a conflict in which many innocent people suffered was not yielding to the powers of darkness, but getting the protagonists to perceive the conflict, their enemy and themselves differently. A genuine peaceful relationship does not come through hatred and violence, although these may bring the fighting to an end; it comes through the *elimination* of hatred and violence.

I was therefore deeply gratified when I realised, a few years ago, that the emphasis had shifted from angry and not infrequently violent demonstrations to conflict resolution, particularly in the form of mediation. As everyone knows, this has now become almost a growth industry. It has penetrated the law, industry, schools, communities, churches, and family relations. Methods and techniques are expounded in countless text books and pamphlets. But is has now swung almost too far in the other direction. Mediation, many feel, is a psycho-social cure-all. Just buy the right book or attend the right study group and you will acquire the equipment to cope with any conflict. There are no losers: everyone can win.

Certainly there are a number of techniques to be learned: how to listen , how to avoid forms of speech which are covertly aggressive (as many of ours are), how to negotiate, how to disagree without offending, how to state a case, etc. However, the most important aspects of mediation, as of other forms of peacemaking, are attitudes of mind, particularly respect, concern and compassion for all other human beings.

I do not know whether to think of these attitudes as being religious, psychological, or moral; different people whom I admire have used all these terms. I personally don't think it matters much. I like to think of these attitudes as simply realistic; human beings are worthy of being considered thus, and if we do so we are more likely to bring about what we are trying to achieve. Without this approach, the process becomes mechanical, a series of gimmicks which ultimately have little significance and may bring the whole activity into disrepute.

I would also stress that it is important that training should usually be followed up. In places where it is urgently requested because people have formidable problems to face, it is especially important: they may need the periodical boost of courage and enthusiasm; they may need more practice and more information; and they may need to talk about recent events with an outsider having a different perspective. But over and beyond this, the trainers, if they do their work properly, become friends with those in their workshops, part of the web of human beings across the globe who are engaged on the same quest. It seems crucial that they should remain in touch.

Part III
Antidote to alienation

Introduction to Part III

Looking back over the ridges of history we can see how the concatenation of circumstances which brought the nation state into
existence has led it forward. The centralisation, the organised armed
forces, the new economic institutions with the new philosophy of
profit, and the surge of technology, swept the nations onwards to the
next ridge: the great surges of colonial and imperial expansion. The
first surge, of course, was to the new world of the Americas. This had
already taken on its own pattern, which has remained distinct in
many ways, by the period of the second surge, which was to India
and the East, while the third, in the latter half of the nineteenth
century, was largely to Africa propelled by Western Europe, and to
Central Asia by Russia.

Now we are poised just over the ridge of decolonisation. It is steep
and sharp, much more precipitous than earlier ridges, squeezed into
the twenty years from 1947 to 1967 and in the former Soviet
Empire into an even shorter period in the early 1990s. In Latin
America there were, of course, virtually no longer any colonies to be
freed from metropolitan control. However, during the great period
of striving for liberation elsewhere, Latin America has been in a
constant turmoil of revolt against oppressive authority.

It is not difficult to see how the anarchic violence and alienation,
which are the subject of this book, emerged from the interactions
which had gone before. It is also not surprising that our efforts to
control a new problem by the methods of an earlier period are
failing. We are actually trying to solve our problems with the intellectual tools, and hence the practical methods, which created them.

It might be argued that the methods are in fact new, since they are
being applied by newly established international agencies. But the
ways of thinking are not. We are stuck in the rut of conventional
concepts of nationhood, state's rights, and diplomatic niceties. In
particular we cannot get away from stereotyped ideas of intervention, and of the relationship of the strong to the weak, whether in
helping them or controlling them.

In this third Part we shall try to suggest a different approach, one
based on the actions and perceptions of a group of people in the
Croatian town of Osijek.

Osijek

When Tito, the President of Yugoslavia, died in 1980, the country was composed of five republics: Slovenia and Croatia which were Catholic and had been a part of the Austro-Hungarian Empire; Serbia which was Orthodox; Montenegro; Macedonia from which the French for fruit salad may well have been derived since it is a great mixture of Albanian, Bulgarian, Greek and other races; and Bosnia Herzogovina which, as we now all know only too well, was a perilous mixture of Muslims, Serbs and Croats. There were also two so-called Autonomous Provinces, Vojvodina, which is largely Hungarian, and Kosovo, where the great majority are Muslim Albanians.

It was widely felt that the country might not remain united after Tito. Its peoples were not all particularly compatible, particularly the Orthodox Serbs and the Catholic Croats. The latter had been established as a puppet state by the Germans during World War II, and its Nazified army, the Ustachas, had massacred members of the Serb resistance, the Chetniks, and their supporters in great numbers. This is strange to look back on as the bulk of the resistance comprised Croats and its leader, Tito, was himself a Croat. It was a situation comparable to that of France, where the forces of Pétain were the creature of the Nazis, who fought against their fellow Frenchmen desperately resisting, under General de Gaulle, the German occupation.

We need not discuss in detail the tangle of potentially explosive relationships in what was Yugoslavia. It is important, however, to realise that there is what might be termed a fault line, both religious and cultural, between the northern republics of Slovenia and Croatia and what lies to the south. The north being Catholic and in the Germanic sphere of cultural influence; the south being Orthodox and deeply affected by the culture of the Ottoman Empire. Along the fault line there has naturally been a considerable mingling of populations through marriage.

Before Yugoslavia dismembered itself, people were not much concerned that one part of their family might be in Croatia and another in Serbia. There were no frontiers to cross, no problems of citizenship or employment. The country was governed by a collective body, the federal presidency comprising the presidents of the five republics. But in the instability following Tito's death and especially change in Eastern Europe, people became uneasy. In addition, those living on the Croatian side (as defined by official frontiers) of the fault line were affected by the old campaign, now whipped up again, for a Greater Serbia comprising all areas with a Serb population.

Competing nationalisms began to develop and to be fomented for reasons which were both economic and political. The people on the whole had had enough of the communism, watered down but still somewhat repressive, of the country. And they were encouraged by what they saw in the rest of Eastern Europe.

On 25 June 1991, both Slovenia and Croatia declared their independence from Yugoslavia. Two days later the Yugoslavian National Army, the JNA, attacked Slovenia. But the war only lasted ten days. The Slovenian response was too vigorous, the JNA detachments were separated from their bases by the whole of now independent Croatia. The soldiers were confused and ashamed by orders to attack what they still thought of as their fellow citizens. Above all, there was no ethnic purpose of the sort which became crucial in both Croatia and Bosnia.

At around the same time, confused fighting involving both Serbian and Croatian paramilitary groups, police and to some extent the JNA broke out in the Croatia-Serbia frontier region.

The fault line runs up from around Knin, where much of the skirmishing occurred, to Osijek, capital of the province of Eastern Slavonia and beyond to Baranja. Osijek lies in the flat Danubian plane in the corner of land where the rivers Drava and Danube meet. It was in this region, around Osijek and Vukovar, that some of the most violent fighting between irregular forces of what was soon to become the Serbo-Croat war occurred.

At first, however, it was a muddled and desperate struggle with many small local groups battling for their own objectives. The role of the JNA was unclear. Was it still the National Yugoslav Army with the duty to keep the country united and prevent internecine hostilities? Or was it in effect the Serbian army which should fight for the declared aims of the Serbian government? (Here I should remind readers that even after the secession of four of the republics, there was still a Yugoslavia composed of the remaining two, powerful Serbia and relatively weak Montenegro. The JNA (largely composed of Serbs) could legitimately still be considered as the Yugoslav army and therefore under the control of Belgrade). Although irregular warfare continued, and in places still does, the JNA, commanded by the notorious Ratko Mladic, was at war with Croatia and engaged in efforts to create the Greater Serbia.

By the time the UN had arranged a cease fire, an area of just under a third of the size of Croatia was under Serb control, and occupied by the United Nations Protection Force (UNPROFOR) with the task of monitoring the cease fire and protecting the delivery of aid where it was needed. The Serbs refer to the territory they have occupied as the Serbian Republic of Krajina. Krajina was originally just the zone around Knin, but the so-called republic extends, with one gap, right up to Osijek and then on to the Hungarian frontier.

From late July until early January 1992, the fighting in these more northerly areas was extremely ferocious. Of the two sizeable towns, Vukovar to the south of Osijek was virtually demolished and fell to the Serbs; Osijek was terribly damaged, suffering about 11,000 casualties of which ten per cent were fatal. In most streets it was impossible to discover a house which had not been damaged; the pock marks of shrapnel were everywhere. I have usually stayed in the apartment of a woman doctor. It is in a tower block and had twice received direct hits. So did the laboratory where she worked in the hospital; since she is a consultant in nuclear medicine, this was very dangerous. Anther house where I stayed once had been rebuilt three times after being bombed — an amazing demonstration of faith!

Unlike Vukovar, Osijek was never overrun. Osijek was brilliantly defended by a man named Branimir Glavas. He has all the qualities of the successful warlord; arrogance, ruthlessness, courage and panache. He is now the governor, the Zupan, of the province.

After the ceasefire on 2 January 1992 the terrible bombardment was greatly reduced. As the director of the hospital told me on my first visit some weeks later, there were only about ten casualties a day now, and two deaths. Some of these were from sniper fire across the Drava which borders the town on one side. This continued until May, when the noise of battle was reduced to occasional rifle shots and automatic fire. The UN told me a year later that there were on average 40 shots exchanged daily in the neighbourhood.

If there were explosions at night it was more likely to be the blowing up either of houses belonging to absent Serbs, or of shops which had not paid their protection dues to the local Mafia which had emerged during the period of greatest violence. This growth of criminality seems easily to develop in such times. It had certainly done so in parts of the Caucasus region.

The population of Osijek is around 100,000 with the addition of 30,000 refugees, some lodging with family members in the town, others in camps around it. Since Osijek was a fault line frontier town, the population was mixed. About twenty per cent were Serbian, and there were a considerable number of Hungarians and some Muslims.

When I was first in Osijek all the children and young people were away. The soaring cathedral was sadly battered. The one plush modern hotel, all plate glass and chrome, had been placed dangerously close to the Drava and was mostly boarded up. The university in the middle of the town, like most other buildings, looked dowdy and neglected with its broken windows and walls splattered with bullet holes. The attractive river walk was still considered dangerous. There was much rejoicing when, a few months later, the situation was considered safe enough for children to return. Their presence added light and civility to a city which, for all its fine eighteenth- and nineteenth-century architecture and spacious well planned public gardens, had seemed grim and threadbare.

Many of the people were still suffering from the shock of the prolonged bombardment, the loss of homes, and the death of family members and friends. The majority were poor and undernourished; food was costly and there were few vegetables, since the previous supply had come mainly from areas now Serb controlled, the so-called UNPAs (UN protected areas). There was massive unemployment because of the destruction of industrial plant.

I should explain how it was that I came to visit Osijek. My wife Anne and I had been asked to attend in March the annual meeting of the Helsinki Citizens Assembly, the non-official arm of the Commission on Security and Cooperation in Europe, to join groups discussing mediation and conflict resolution. In one of these groups was a delightful and articulate Croatian woman, Vesna Terselic, from Zagreb. She was very active in the cause of peace and had set up Anti Ratna Kampgne (ARK), the anti-war campaign. This was a brave thing do to in a country inflamed and angry from attacks upon it, and one in which the civil rights of protesters were not too well defined.

She told us that some people in Osijek were planning to establish a branch of ARK and intended to launch it with a series of public meetings, seminars and discussions in April. We were all invited to attend. In fact two friends of mine did so, one who had also been at the conference, and one from the Bradford University department of peace studies. We were joined in Zagreb by Erich Bachmann, an American peace worker living in Germany, and three from Zagreb ARK, Vesna, Aida Bagic, and a Dutch volunteer. We supped together and next morning went by train to Osijek, an trip of about four and a half hours. This was longer than it could have been, but the direct line had run through a chunk of now occupied country.

As one approaches Osijek the rail and the road traffic pass through a corridor between the surrounding UNPAs. The smashed new post office building faced arrivals at the station. It had been unwisely — as it turned out, but who could have foretold the coming rain of bombs? — constructed mainly of glass. It seemed to me a symbol of the town's agony. Now it has been rebuilt. A symbol of hope? Or of vain optimism?

The people

We were welcomed in the most friendly fashion by some of the people who were planning to set up the peace group. They took us to lunch at the hospital where one of them worked, Katarina Kruhonja, whom I referred to before. Later we had a formal meeting with the director, and were then shown around the underground ward.

Katarina, with a man, Krunoslav Sukic, were the leading spirits of the embryonic peace movement. She is a catholic and he an atheist, but they are in complete and harmonious accord that the movement must have a nonviolent character. Indeed, it would be fair to say that they were the movement. A few others were interested and friendly; two or three of these had come to greet us at the station, but were not so deeply committed. Many more, including most of Katarina's medical colleagues, were hostile; Kruno, a social philosopher, had himself been unemployed for some time because of his unpopular views.

Fortunately Katarina was to be the hostess of myself and Aida, who spoke perfect English which Katarina, at that stage, did not. We climbed (the electricity for the lift was off) to her apartment on the ninth of the ten floors in a tower block. There we had the first of our countless talks. These have usually been at night, after the day's work, and early in the morning (over last night's washing up) before the next day's engagements.

Katarina had been deeply distressed not only by the death and devastation of the attack on Osijek, but by the effect that this had had on the psychological climate. Fear and anger were to be expected, but these were now coupled with demonisation of the enemy and acceptance of the logic of war as the sole means of survival. At the same time there were urgent tasks in caring for those maimed in mind or body by the bombardment, and or the 30,000 people, displaced from their homes in the by then Serb-occupied areas, who had flooded into the town. But when she and Kruno, who shared her feelings, discussed their views, they met with almost universal hostility. How could they even for a moment consider any course of action except to win back the land they had lost; and how could this be done without fighting?

Serbs with whom they shared the whole area of Eastern Slavonia became devils overnight. Those who actually lived in Osijek in their thousands, who were Croatian citizens, and were by no means Serb nationalists, were ostracised, dismissed from their jobs and later evicted from their homes.

A further element of social pathology was growing with sinister speed: criminality. As I mentioned before, in times of disturbance — especially where guns abound — this virus seeps in through the widening cracks in the social order.

Katarina, I think, was even more upset by the poisoned minds than by the wounded bodies. How could the semblance of peace ever be restored when people were dominated by such venomous feelings?

The people of Osijek, even those so intelligent and generally sophisticated as Katarina, were far behind those of West Europe and America in their understanding of the issues of peace and violence. In London, Bradford, and Cambridge, Massachusetts where I had lived for the past few decades, we had wrestled with them constantly. We had debated and demonstrated over the questions of nuclear danger and disarmament, the Cold War, and the Vietnam War. We had studied and sometimes worked with the prophets of the age, Mahatma Gandhi, J.P. Narayan, Martin Luther King, Cezar Chavez, Danilo Dolci.

But Katarina and her friends and opponents, living in a communist society, although a somewhat dissident one, knew virtually nothing of all this. Moreover, as someone put it to me, Osijek is a provincial city, literally very much at the end of the line from any centre of cosmopolitan culture.

When I first met Katarina and Kruno they had, I think, only recently come across the word 'nonviolence'. However, it had immediately resonated excitingly in her mind. Although she questioned me at length about it, tentatively, and saying how little she knew, I could see at once that in the depths of her heart she knew all about it. She has a deep relisgious faith from which quite naturally flows a creatively compassionate nature which recognises the divine in everyone.

With a handful of collaborators, she and Kruno had planned the launch to which the other visitors and I had been invited. Vesna too had been very helpful. The launch consisted of two or three rather formal discussions with perhaps thirty people: teachers in the university (where we met), members of various civic and educational bodies, and social workers. As far as I can remember (and I didn't hear everything either) these were not particularly controversial — more civil exchanges of view than anything else, but the underlying tensions occasionally surfaced.

There were also seminars led by us, the visitors. One was on medical and another on educational issues. I facilitated one on mediation. There were about fifteen people, including Aida as interpreter. I had already discovered at the HCA conference in Bratislava that no one really knew what mediation was but felt it was some sort of mysterious technique for solving all problems of conflict.

Their attitude reminded me of the Ghanaian villagers who thought in the same way about injections. If they went to hospital and came away without a jab, even after they had been given a pill or a bottle of medicine, they felt cheated. But there was a kind man outside the hospital with a hypodermic syringe and a bowl of dirty water who, for a moderate fee, would satisfy their needs. I was placed in the role of the man with the bowl and syringe. There was some disappointment, most politely expressed, when it became clear that mediation was not the expected panacea.

Mediation, of course, requires two protagonists whom the mediator can try to bring together. Naturally in Osijek, there were a number of people and groups who disliked each other; for example, Glavas whom I have already mentioned, the authoritarian Zupan, and Zlatko Kramaric, the mayor who was a liberal and had a PhD in Macedonian poetry. Moreover, the cliques and enmities in the town were complex and interwoven, but did not affect feelings about the common monolithic foe, the Serbs.

And there was no obvious way of mediating from a provincial base about an international matter. Anyway it was impossible practically; there was no contact between the people of Osijek and those of the surrounding UNPAs. The frontier was guarded by the UN and even if it had been possible to cross, it would have been extremely dangerous (though as we shall see later an alternative procedure was developed). But, in any case, the potential outcomes even from successful mediation were not really attractive to most people: either to resume hostilities, or to return to their old homes (provided they had not been taken over by Serbs) under continued UN protection in a country still Serb dominated. In fact hardly anyone, Croat or, I think, Serb, was willing to consider compromise, which is, of course, the prerequisite of mediation.

The ambiguous and difficult role of the UN is worth mentioning.

It was quite differently conceived by the two parties (note that the situation was not the same as that which developed later in Bosnia). The Croatians felt that the UN's task was to evict the Serbs from the area of Croatia that they had occupied, so that they, the rightful Croatian inhabitants, could return and take over control once more.

The Serbs thought that its task was to prevent the Croatians from returning. Both were disappointed. The UN neither tried to oust the Serbs, nor did it (at that stage) actively discourage the Croats from planning their return. In fact the first few times I visited Osijek the return of a thousand people was being considered. Katarina with some others, including myself, had discussions with the senior police officer who would have been responsible for the conduct of the march home. He was cautiously exploring the idea of having them trained in methods which were low-keyed and unconfrontational. We offered to arrange for policemen who had had this sort of training at Bradford to come out to Osijek, and a very senior retired chief constable volunteered his services.

In the end, however, the UN vetoed the whole idea of the march home; they considered it too dangerous. This in fact illustrates their mandated role, which was to prevent the outbreak of further violence by diplomacy and persuasion and any other method not involving force or even a remote suggestion of force.

It might be argued that their mandate should have been different. If the UN had charged in with guns blazing as they did in Korea, some would have been very happy, and some miserable. However, this time Security Council instructions were quite different — and much more difficult for soldiers to follow; but they did so with reticence, skill and sensitivity. And everyone hated them for it. Round the UNPROFOR headquarters in Zagreb is a wall of bricks each inscribed with the name of someone killed, it is believed, through the inactivity of the UN.

This, my first visit to Osijek lasted less than a week. I left with a feeling of dissatisfaction. I had been there long enough to develop a great regard and liking for Katarina, Kruno and some of the others. But I felt I was leaving unfinished work behind. I told Katarina I would be happy to return fairly soon at a time when things were less hectic with seminars (which hadn't worked out very well!) and public occasions, so that we could talk more and explore the possibility that I could make some useful contribution.

Katarina felt this would be a good idea, and I returned in about a month to give an informal seminar/ workshop to a group of people she knew. We thought the best approach would be to talk and feel our way into and around the types of situations which can arise, and had indeed arisen, in embattled places like Osijek.

The early days of the centre

I returned to Osijek in June. I had given a good deal of thought to what we might do in the workshop that Katarina had organised. I had given a number of workshops on mediation, but this was different. What might be helpful to people who might be faced with the multifarious problems of crisis and chaos, problems I could only envisage in a most general way? The main feature of the context in which we would be operating was violence, so the focus of the workshop should be nonviolence. But nonviolence training is a very idiosyncratic business. I tried to understand what would be most useful to help a group of young people (to those in their late seventies anyone under fifty-five is young), who were facing almost any imaginable exigency, to function best both as individuals and as members of a team.

A facile answer would be to list the qualities to develop. But how to develop them when listed? I would prefer to think that what is needed, and is always needed by all of us, is the fullest possible development of our humanity, our potential as human beings. This means becoming able to escape from the mindless automatism that governs so much of our lives, from senseless worries and fears, from prejudice, from ego cherishing and irritability, from vanity, from illusions of guilt and badness, from belief in separate existence. These and all other negative emotions are like a fist tightly closed around the heart. They imprison our consciousness within the narrow confines of the self. But to be fully human our consciousness must expand, gradually embracing all others, including all nonhuman others with whom we share the planet. It means losing the lonely sense of separation. It means to be rather than to do.

But pondering these ideas, I thought, how could I profess to 'teach' others to be more human? I would have to be as much as I was expecting others to be. The answer, it seemed to me, was to use the workshop for sharing and mutual help; the learning would come to all of us from this, rather than from any formal instruction. In fact, the first lesson would be that we all have something to give and something to learn.

I felt, however, that there would be need for some loose and probably overlapping sequence of emphases in our exploration. This is how it worked out:

Using the metaphor of the fist around the heart we considered the things that made it tighter or looser; for example, what threw us off balance and what made us more confident. We tried various awareness and listening exercises. Also I emphasised that I believed in the essential soundness of our nature, saying that in my experience if we approached people with respect and expecting them to behave decently, it would evoke their better nature. But if one expected the worst, one would find it.

Moving on from this, but on the same track, we tried to become aware of some of our blind spots, prejudices, irrational reactions including anxieties, dislikes and guilt; things that could impair our judgement and our relations with colleagues and others.

We considered our interconnectedness with all human beings, with all life, with the planet. In so doing we examined and tried to rid ourselves of conventional views of completely dichotomised self and other, friend and enemy.

We traced the connections between what we had been discovering and different facets of violent situations; we explored these from human, economic and political points of view, considering refugees, homelessness, psychological and physical traumas of war, separation of families, social dislocation, deprivation, and poverty. All of these were, of course, examined in the context of Osijek as well as generally.

We learned something of the basic principles and practices of nonviolent protest and conflict resolution and thought about their application in particular situations.

Throughout we devised what seemed to be appropriate role plays and other exercises.

The workshop lasted five days and about twenty people came. Since some were working, they could not all come all the time, but attendance was generally very good. We met for the first four days in a room loaned to us by a charity but they needed it on the last day, so we migrated to a garish disco, incongruously located in a picturesque building in the old town.

Most of the members of the workshop had either not met before, or knew each other only slightly. They came as individuals, rather than as members of an existing group. But it was noticeable that a warm and cooperative atmosphere developed very soon.

About half way through the meetings, a very significant thing happened. Individuals who had mainly talked about 'I' and 'me' began to talk about what 'we' should do, how 'we' should arrange the next meeting, who should take notes, send out invitations, and so on. It seemed that, without anyone making a specific proposal, everyone had reached an unspoken agreement that we formed the nucleus of a group which would do the things we had been discussing.

This was exciting and encouraging.

I should add that I am rather embarrassed at saying so much about the workshop that I facilitated. Many other people have given other sorts of training and I believe that it is important to maintain a flow of learning/teaching experiences where difficult and stressful work is being carried out; workshops provide a combination of stimulus and the relaxation of standing back from the demands of a crisis. I mention my own experience because it is the one I know most about; readers may care to compare it with those mentioned in an earlier chapter.

Human rights

During the summer of 1992 the Centre for Peace, Nonviolence and Human Rights, launched in May, came into existence physically in a couple of rooms off the cloister of a former monastery.

Initially Katarina, Kruno and the other centre members (most of the people who had attended the seminar) considered that the main function of the centre could be described as educational. There were some refugee children for whom there were no educational facilities available. There was also a need to introduce peace education into the system. And there was an even greater if more nebulous need to educate people in general on the meaning of peace and nonviolence. Human rights were not referred to in the centre's name at this stage.

But no one had foreseen that human rights issues would force their way so swiftly and imperatively onto the agenda. It might, however, have been anticipated that in such times of chauvinistic and authoritarian domination, it is the misfits and minorities who are persecuted. In this case, of course, it was particularly the Serbs, who comprised twenty per cent of the population of Osijek. As the centre became better known, so complaints of human rights violations first trickled, then flooded in to it. They concerned issues of citizenship rights, employment and, most numerous and most crucial, cases of eviction from their apartments of people with Serb connections of one sort or another.

Most of the latter involved former members of the JNA, which was associated with Serbia whether or not the actual members were Serb. They were evicted or threatened with eviction to make way for serving soldiers of the Croatian army. Informed legal experts confirmed that this was not lawful; nevertheless the official responsible was himself a judge. This collusion of the legal system with ethnic repression had made attorneys reluctant to take such law suits, and had created among the people a great mistrust of the local courts. However, centre members would form teams to offer non-violent protection to threatened families, confronting and reasoning with the military who came to carry out the evictions. Usually these measures succeeded in at least delaying the procedure.

One day, however, things went wrong. The military came and after talking with the centre members, went away. The centre members then left, except for one who was not quite satisfied that the soldiers would not return. Which they did, and beat and evicted the inhabitants.

The next day Katarina and Kruno went to confront the judge responsible. He accused them of being unpatriotic and traitorous. The military, he said, were incensed with them and he had had to restrain them from taking action. If however they were to continue their offensive activities, he would not answer for the consequences.

I arrived in Osijek the day after this frightening meeting. We talked for a long time about what could be done. They rejected the idea of giving up the human rights protection, saying that to do so would be to rip out the moral guts of their work. However, there were various ways of proceeding less provocatively: appealing to responsible people locally and internationally, reporting and monitoring breaches of human rights, enlisting the help of the clergy, and initiating a national debate on the issue.

After several weeks of effort and worry, the threat to Katarina and Kruno seemed to recede. Indeed, as more and more people in Croatia and internationally came to know about and admire the centre's work, the authorities gained a certain measure of reflected glory from it.

The human rights programme is now both sizeable and effective with a full-time lawyer who provides legal counsel and advocacy, legal representation, advice for conscientious objectors and data collection. A training programme for human rights officers is being launched and will constitute one of many filaments linking the centre with other groups nationally and internationally.

Education

Educational activities come in three main strands. The first has just been mentioned: training for human rights workers.

The second is training, and training trainers, to be active in the field of nonviolent action for social change. This is carried out in the Peace Education Centre. Besides active work on specific issues, this centre helps train citizens' and women's groups; teachers who wish to learn about peace education, creativity through play and multicultural education; those in the healing and caring services who need to understand the impact of social factors on their work; and members of the public interested in learning about human rights and freedom, democracy and responsibility, and about living non-violently (which is being done through panel discussions, round tables and publications).

The third educational strand is to do with teachers who are themselves displaced persons and who, like their students, have experienced the traumas of war. They go through a training which it is hoped will help them and those they teach to overcome the social and emotional handicaps and blockages which their hardships may have induced. The character of the workshops involved is not different in kind from those we have already considered, but they include more of what is specifically peace education — how to heal and to help, and to resolve painful tensions.

Having completed their preparation, the teachers go into the schools in and around Osijek to give workshops based on what they themselves have learned. So far 30 teachers have given 720 workshops in more than 10 schools to over 1000 children. These are reported to have been very rewarding and the school administrations have been cooperative.

Displaced persons

Much of the work of the Centre for Peace, Nonviolence and Human Rights concerns displaced persons and refugees.

In one camp the centre is promoting market gardening by providing large numbers of glasshouses and promoting a market for the sale of produce.

Another project which combines therapeutic value with economic opportunity is a series of courses in sewing and tailoring for women. Several hundred women have been through these courses which, they say, are 'bringing them back to life'.

A third project concerns the displaced inhabitants of a village, Laslovo, in the UNPA Zone East. This village was entirely destroyed and its Hungarian-speaking people all fled to nearby Osijek. Money is being collected for rebuilding purposes in the event of their return. (Unlike in other areas, the destruction means that they would not find their homes occupied by Serbs.) Perhaps more important are the efforts being made to adjust them to the idea of living together in relative harmony with the Serb people who drove them out. This of course has significant implications for their lives wherever they may be.

External relations of the centre

The Laslovo village project is a joint effort between the centre and the citizens of Wageningen in the Netherlands, which is twinned with Laslovo. This relationship has also encouraged the Council of Europe to establish one of its Embassies of Local Democracy in the city. It has also spurred the centre to create a channel of communication with some of the Serb population in the same area as the village.

Relations with the neighbouring Serb occupied areas, the UNPAs — geographically adjacent, yet politically and psychologically so distant — are a matter of great concern for the future when the state of war with Serbia has passed. It is at present almost impossible for anyone from Croatia to go there directly, but efforts are constantly being made to communicate with people there. Sometimes old friends, or family members separated by war, are able to get together in neighbouring Hungarian towns such as Mohacs or Pecs.

It is, however, not impossible for Croatians to visit Serbia and to make contact with individuals and with the peace groups which are springing up in various places. The emergence of these groups in parts of former Yugoslavia is a sign of encouragement for the future.

In the summer of 1994 the centre organised a successful course in Mohacs for young people from Serbia, Osijek and Western Europe (particularly the Netherlands). This was certainly important and enlightening for the participants, but also for Croatia. At first there was a howl from the right-wing press of Osijek making the familiar accusations of traitorous lack of patriotism. But a group of young people made a firm statement to their interviewers. They told them that it must be understood that they, the younger generation, belonged to the post-communist era; they stood for friendship and reconciliation, rather than hatred and violence. This episode triggered healthy nationwide debate.

Many of the centre members travel a good deal. (Of these about fifty, mostly women, are the core members who make the plans and devise the strategy; a rather larger number work mainly on specific projects.) They have given or attended workshops, and in general taken an active part in creating the network of groups and individuals who are working positively to reduce violence and promote a generously peaceful atmosphere. For example, during the year in which I am writing I have met Katarina in Sweden and Spain and should have met her a third time in Scotland, but returned too late from Osijek — where of course I had also been working with her.

In the summer of 1993, to celebrate their survival and their birthday as an organisation, they organised a great week of 'Peace and Culture'. This was held in the area of the old monastery where they were then located (now they have more spacious and modern — but less picturesque — quarters). There were serious talks and debates, exhibitions, performances by the children, parties, music, poetry and dancing, meditation and feasts. Everything was open to the town and large numbers of people came enthusiastically, as did about twenty foreign guests. It was a wonderful occasion.

Two things impressed me particularly. The monastery was next door to a military headquarters, from which suspicion if not hostility might have been expected. But no. One day they gave us all lunch!

The other thing was the beauty and light-hearted cheerfulness of the women. I asked them how, in the face of danger and the terrible threats they had endured, they could appear so untouched, so merry. They answered, 'We were faced with a terrifying choice. When we chose to face the terror rather than to dilute our principles, we felt liberated.'

Assessment

The genesis of the idea for a centre came late in 1991, when Katarina and Kruno, horrified by the violent and militaristic atmosphere, began to speculate on alternative responses to the situation. They were revolting against the growing alienation that violence creates and that in turns creates more violence. It is an automatic, completely unaware response, in the sense I give to unawareness. It is the response of people who are blind with anger, or fear, or grief, or hatred, or all four, and who in consequence become estranged, alienated from parts of their background, their society, themselves.

When I mentioned alienation recently to a friend, he asked me, 'Alienation from what?' I paused, wondering if I had used the word too glibly, then realised that I meant it in a most profound sense: estrangement from life, from the world of the living, a descent into the realm of death, disaster and despair.

Consider the alienated killers, whether sadistic murderers in Bosnia and Liberia, or the five young teenagers I read of this morning in England who knifed to death a blind old man, and later listened impassively as the charges were read. These are people who have nothing but their terrible compulsions; no ambitions, no hopes, no faith in anything, no sense of their own reality, no guidelines of morality. They are alienated from society, of course, but from themselves as living creatures, from everything alive.

It would clearly be a gross exaggeration to suggest that there are many people like this, but plainly the number is growing. When the milieu is openly and horribly violent, the growth is more speedy. I have spent long periods in areas of great violence. Usually I have found that humane and decent people would start by avoiding being judgemental or angry about insurgents or others the government was fighting. However, they gradually tended to became hard and callous. (I must say that I have not found this in Ireland nor, as I have described, in Nigeria.)

The centre's work as an antidote to alienation

I do not think that Katarina and her companions actually thought of their work in these terms. However, they greatly disliked the atmosphere in Osijek and wanted to show that the continued expression of vengeful hatred was doing no good to anyone; that what was needed instead of the militaristic bombast was getting down to the job of helping the victims of the war, completely irrespective of their ethnic origin. And this they proceeded to do.

At the same time as they were building up the centre, they were thinking constantly about the meaning of nonviolence. What does nonviolent help mean? Surely more than just providing what is needed to alleviate some hardship or disadvantage. They came to understand that in all human relationships there is a chance to give help at a variety of levels. The crudest level is purely material: providing the bread or the bed. But at another level we can provide solace and affection, and advice if needed on how to tackle difficult problems. At a yet higher level it is possible that the act of giving can include provision of stimulation and/or the opportunity for the recipient to do something which will contribute positively to the situation in which they suffered need. Maybe they will join one of the centre's projects, or in some other way help to maintain or rebuild the civil society. All this helps to restore meaning to life, a sense of hope and purpose which is nourished both by the formal activities of the centre and by the personal contacts and the friendships which have flowered between those engaged in the common enterprise.

Apart from those few who may still see the centre as a threat to their war mentality, the Osijek community values and trusts it as an organisation that is doing good and has no power or party political axes to grind. It is recognised as having no doctrinal bias beyond a compassionate concern for human well-being.

The centre members have close and friendly relationships with a number of other bodies, such as those set up among the communities of displaced persons, but are also themselves setting up new institutions. These, without any particular effort being made, embody the nonviolent ethos of the centre. Such a group is that of the Laslovo community, and those associated with the Peace Education Centre and with the various social/economic enterprises which have been established for the refugees and displaced persons. These developments have not been exactly planned, but have coalesced out of the association of people with common interests and common purposes.

If one has to define the nature of the centre, I suppose one would have to say that it is a non-governmental organisation, an NGO. But this would give a false impression. Most of the myriad NGOs exist primarily for a particular purpose: to care for some aspect of health, the environment, education, welfare of the old, animals, children, victims of famine or oppression, etc., etc. But this centre, which came into existence to demonstrate a different way of reacting to a violent situation, is expanding into the entire realm of human life to find ways of solving every human problem and healing every human pain of which they become aware.

The extent of this expansion cannot wholly be explained, it seems to me, from the effect of what the centre members are heard to say or seen to do in relation to particular difficulties and problems. It is more the effect of what they are, of the qualities that are evoked and nourished by their awareness. This has spread like leaven through the community, changing it; to use another metaphor, it is the anti-dote to the death-dealing virus of alienation.

People

You may feel that what I have written is extravagant, or conversely that the people I am talking about are super women and men. I would answer that they are indeed fine people, but neither saints nor geniuses. They are simply human beings who have gone a long way towards realising the universal human potentials for wisdom, courage and compassion. Some whom I have known from the first days of our association have grown in a manner which I find both encouraging and inspiring. They were good people, but some of them worried, frightened and unsure; now they are strong, cheerful, effective, most attractive and delightful. I have never met a collection of people whom I both loved and respected so much.

Thinking about them as I write, I cease to be amazed at what they have achieved; people like that can do anything.

My memories of one woman epitomise my feelings for them all. At the centre's festival for peace and culture in 1993, this woman, with a German visitor, gave a most moving and beautiful meditation with readings and quiet song. The next evening a lively group of young local musicians performed; she jumped onto the platform and did a wild bacchanalian dance. Her combination of the spiritual with the earthy represents my feelings about many of them.

I would like to write a lot about Katarina, but am afraid of embar-rassing her. I will only say that it was she who set the stage intellectually and I would add spiritually, because she has a quality that goes far beyond intellectual ability, for all the developments we have been considering. The best way I can describe this quality is to use Gandhi's phrase, 'soul truth', a phrase which implies both power and rightness.

The centre and peace

The prime purpose of the centre is peace, the establishment of peaceful relations at all levels; peace is the first descriptive word in its title. There is little it can do in relation to the existing state of war between Croatia and Serbia. The only thing possible is, to some extent, to mitigate the fever of violence in one small area. There is a continual quiet effort to probe through the barriers of suspicion into Serbia and to build relations with individuals and groups there. However, even if this is allowed to continue unabated, it could be years before the general climate of opinion is sufficiently changed to affect the governments concerned.

What seems to me extremely important, however, is that the work of the centre is to both stimulate and preserve the values on which harmony can eventually be restored. Respect for human life, concern for the other, the de-demonisation of the enemy, concern for justice, sensitivity to the great variety of pains are essential if a state of non-war is to be transformed into a truly peaceful relationship in which the other person is cherished to the point where they become the same.

This is the constant and all-pervading thrust of the centre's work. It serves as a repository for all those attitudes, so damaged in the fury of militarism, upon which peace depends. When the fighting stops and the peace accords are signed, bitter feelings may well continue to ruin the future with poisons of the past. However, to the extent that bodies like the centre and its equivalents which are springing up in many areas of former Yugoslavia have retained the values of peace, real harmony may come with the political decision to end the war.

This is a hope on which to pin our faith; a reason for giving all the support we can to these brave groups which have resisted the dangerous hostility of the violent without the degradation of hating them.

It is hardly necessary to say that Osijek should not be taken as a universal model. Different cultures, different conflicts and different levels of material development will demand different varieties of antidote to violence. Given the essential foundation of loving respect for human life, for peace and for justice, a great variety of approaches to meeting human needs and establishing civil society will be relevant and effective.

It is also clear that what I have related is only the first chapter, the opening of consciousness, the awakening of a new awareness. Ahead lies the vital question of how these largely inward developments can be reified within the framework of appropriate policies and structures: legal, social, economic and political. Many authors have tried to write these chapters in their own idioms; the marxists, Margaret Thatcher and her sort and the fascists are just a contemporary sample. But their first chapters, beguiling as they may once have seemed, were faulty and things went terribly wrong. The societies which they had hoped to create became monstrous, cruel, corrupt — and inefficient.

My friends in Osijek have, I believe, written an impeccable first chapter. I have no detailed idea of how the book will continue, but I believe that some of the arrangements they have made to implement their ideas promisingly adumbrate subsequent chapters. I hope to live to read some of the future instalments.

Implications

It would have been unnecessary for me to write these pages if the great international agencies, especially the United Nations, had not failed to hold back the floods of violence throughout the world. I must emphasise, however, that it is not the organisation itself that I am criticising; many of its officials are brilliant and dedicated women and men who have done great work for humanity. No, it is the member states. These, particularly the Security Council members, all too often seem more concerned to safeguard and promote their own national interests than to protect those of others. It must be admitted, in addition, that 'modern' violence, so anarchic and pointless, expressing so desperate an alienation, is incredibly hard to cope with.

A new role for the UN

We have, I think, learned that the use of force tends simply to pile more violence on violence, but what else are we to do? Certainly the use of UN forces in any capacity is fraught with difficulty: in Bosnia they are reviled for either using too little force or too much, and either way their presence hasn't made the situation much better. They have bravely and skilfully helped with the delivery of aid, but UNHCR officials told me that they were doing all right before the arrival of the military. Although they have been useful in many respects, they have also brought fresh difficulties — an additional group of armed men added an imponderable element to the explosive situation, a new potential enemy for either or both sides. But what alternatives are there?

We have to think of new functions for the UN. This is always difficult in any context. We are reluctant to give up the security of the past — just as the French relied on a World War I type of defence, the useless Maginot Line. Just as, in the political field, the UN and EU negotiators relied on the promises of people to whom truth and falsity were significant tactically but not morally.

The first change, then, would be to limit the use by the UN of military forces very considerably. Their military role might perhaps be confined to observation (as in the Middle East and the Karakoram), and to a small emergency force for the rescue or protection of uninvolved people in crisis areas. This does not imply, however, that the UN should be no longer involved in peace making activities. On the contrary, it should be more and more intensively concerned with forestalling the outbreak of violence, and reducing or ending it if it has started.

This, of course, is already done by diplomacy, but I am suggesting that the use of nonviolence workshops or seminars (and indeed the type of seminar I described in Osijek) can contribute to changes of perception that reduce the likelihood of violence. In addition, mediation, both hard and soft, can achieve the same ends as diplomatic negotiation, but with a more stable psychological basis. The reason for this is that mediation should bring about a certain shift in attitude, whereas solutions reached through negotiation may be simply expedient and not imply any change of heart. And this is the crux of peace. There must be a change of heart. Without this no settlement can be considered secure.

Preconflict work will be greatly facilitated if UN (or other) workers can manage to identify local people through whom to work. This, I am convinced by my own time in Osijek, is most desirable. The people of the area are the only ones who can really deal with the problems of that area; they know the language, the culture, the hopes and fears, the dangers and difficulties, they know and are committed to the *people*.

And this is a further suggested shift for UN policy: to build many more and much closer relations with the *peoples* whom it is supposed to represent.

It may probably not be easy for them to practice the mediation methods which it is to be hoped they have learned in workshops, while large-scale fighting is in progress; major decisions will be made by politicians in the administrative centres. However, in times of stress local tensions and injustices are apt to emerge, and in cases of general breakdown, mediation may become very important.

Regional agencies

One handicap of the UN is its size and its diversity. Even a regional body, such as the OAU, is too large for efficiency, while the difference between North and Sub-Saharan Africa is too great for easy agreement on complex issues. Thus I would be inclined to advocate an Organisation of Sub-Saharan African Unity (OSSAU) for that region, and perhaps another comprising North Africa and the Middle East. I don't want to go further into controversial and, for our purposes, irrelevant details, but would like to suggest that pre-violence and mediation training might be best carried out *in the affected localities.* Certainly, as we have seen, there are specifically African approaches to peacemaking, just as there are Muslim ones now being very effectively practised by wise, prudent and tradition-ally restrained elders in Kosovo.

Some kind of regional authority is also, I am sure, even more appropriate for development. The African disaster, in which war, famine, and fatuous and/or exploitative policies are inextricably interconnected, can only be handled by Africans. However, a part of the problem is related to the local rivalries and suspicions. Therefore, although the continent's difficulties must be coped with by its own people, some balance and dispassion should be exercised by outsiders. But *not* from Europe or North America; the further that white people from the rich nations can be distanced from develop-ment issues in the Third World, the better — at least until the image of arrogantly omniscient neocolonialist experts has faded from memory. However, perhaps it might be that a Union of South and South-Eastern Asia should also supply delegates to the OSSAU.

The immediate future

I began this chapter by discussing some very major changes that are, of course, the least likely to come about, at least in the immediate future. There are, however, a number of things to be done — and some of them are being done — today. These will tend to push things in the direction I have suggested.

Firstly, there are a number of organisations which are carrying out the training I have referred to. (I mention only two that I have been directly involved with; there are others no doubt equally significant, but I do not feel qualified to discuss them.) One is the Global Alliance of Peace Services (GAPS). Its name accurately suggests its purpose: to form a consortium of NGOs which are concerned to train people for action in times of turmoil or disaster, and to provide for monitoring, as it already has done for the South African elections. Trainings have taken place in both Sweden and South Africa with Swedish, South African and other participants, and a team of observers for the South African elections was also organised. The second is the Coordinating Committee for Conflict Resolution Training in Europe (CCCRTE). This was set up after the first few visits to Osijek to provide for a continuation of work there and in other places in Europe, mainly in former Yugoslavia, although some related work has been carried out in the North Caucasus area and in other

regions. The membership of CCCRTE is largely drawn from representatives of international NGOs — Peace Brigades International,
War Resisters International, International Fellowship of
Reconciliation, Quaker Peace and Service, Bradford University Centre
for Conflict Resolution, Responding to Conflict, and a few others.

I need not say any more about CCCRTE; its work is illustrated by
the developments in Osijek. But I would like to emphasise the nature
of the role of people such as myself. Although I am proud that the
centre appointed me as their external advisor, it was as an expression
of friendship rather than a reflection of my role. I saw my main task
as being to give moral support and encouragement, to discuss any
issue that might interest or worry them, and to help them to do and
to have what was necessary: I would, for example, carry out cash
which has been subscribed for their work, or a lap-top computer, or
some particular medicine. I might raise the money for a fax machine,
or put them in touch with people in comparable situations elsewhere
with whom they could usefully exchange experiences, or arrange for
centre members to go to meetings or conferences in other countries.
But I never told them what I thought they ought to do. I was well
aware that they knew this better than I did.

I would like to stress strongly at this point the advantages of doing
work under the aegis of an NGO; even if one is working alone (as I
have sometimes done, though I don't advise it for practical and
emotional reasons) some affiliation is desirable. However, even the
most benevolent government is under suspicion because politicians,
as a breed, are seldom trusted. The UN itself is often unpopular, as
is now the case in former Yugoslavia, despite the visibly splendid
work of the UNHCR.

But NGOs, being the creatures of neither governments nor UN,
and doing a job out of concern and care rather than for profit, are
usually acceptable (though this is not always the case in Africa:
Rwanda, for example, is overrun by NGOs having the most trivial
and unnecessary objectives).

I should add another reason for operation under the umbrella of
NGOs. They provide a conveniently indirect conduit along which a
small contribution can be made to a good cause without creating any
political embarrassment. I say a 'small' amount, because the costs
are really not big: we operate far below the opulence level of the
average international 'expert' or 'advisor', or that of a Member of
Parliament on a 'fact finding mission'.

I hope all people engaged in this work may be able to influence
their governments, as well as the relevant branches of the UN, to

recognise the approach to peace work I have been trying to advance: through unofficial bodies (with or without a modicum of official support) who are facilitating local peace groups in their campaign against violence.

And I further hope that this will lead them to advocate changing the peacemaking policies of the UN and other international bodies. To this end I must mention an encouraging recent development: the Council of Europe has created Local Democracy Embassies to towns which expressed enthusiasm for the idea. Osijek is one such town. The role of these embassies is as yet not clearly defined, but within my limited experience, they are extremely supportive of what is suggested here.

A middle way

Like other people of my age, I have been impelled to change my opinions about almost everything on which I ever had an opinion. I think I now understand a little of what the Buddha meant when he said when asked his views on something or other, 'The Venerable One has no opinions on anything'. He meant that he *knew*. Of course, I do not claim to know in this sense, but I recognise that what I may think today about this or that, I may not think tomorrow when I have more information or am in a different mood. But some things I do make bold to say I know at least partially, because this knowledge has passed the test of long experience.

One such thing relates to violence: violence is born of the illusion that good, that is to say basically love, happiness and enlightenment, may come from it.

Another illusion is that human beings who do what we call bad things, such as violent acts, are themselves bad: they are misled, misinformed and unskilled in the conduct of life.

A third thing is that violence lies not so much in action as in a state of mind: it is ultimately the violence of the heart rather than of the body which damages us.

A fourth thing is that we are all of the same nature, though our experiences may have shaped it differently; therefore it is not for us to put ourselves above or below other human beings, but to love and cherish them as ourselves.

These understandings will, I believe, help us to steer a course between several sets of destructive poles in our human relations and our peacemaking.

One is between intense involvement (often coupled with harmful interference) on the one side, and impassivity and lack of interest on the other. The first may lead to confusing and disempowering the very people one wishes to help; the second, to neglect opportunities to help. I have hinted at the alternative middle way in speaking of our relationship with the people of Osijek; it is one based on mutual respect and affection. We value and admire what they are trying to do; they appreciate our help and goodwill.

Another set of poles are intellectual arrogance and abject humility. These constitute a complete antithesis to the Buddha's teaching. Extremes of pride and abasement are fruit of equally damaging egoic illusions. I have met plenty of both, a source of extreme irritation to their colleagues, and a serious hindrance to effective work. The illusions woven around pride impede a genuine appreciation of the situation, while excessive humility acts as a brake on important discussions.

Thus, in so many respects, what we can do for other people depends on what we can do for ourselves, which is — primarily — to see ourselves, and hence others, as we truly are. The more we can do this, the more we can escape from the binding illusions of the past: that peace can come from unpeace; that love of country justifies hatred of people; that our enemies are, ipso facto, evil.

Conclusion: Transformation through shared humanity

Since I began writing these pages in November 1994, a number of events have occurred which were of significance for what we have been discussing.

Some of these have been good: the strengthening of the great South African transformation; the cautious moves towards peace in Northern Ireland; the apparent end of the war in Angola.

Some have been bad: Boris Yeltsin's foul-tempered assault on Chechnya, a loathsome sequel to his attack on his own parliament building; the former Rwanda army composed of Hutus, presently in refugee camps across the border, plotting to resume the conflict; so far as I know all other wars are still continuing.

One of the most vicious of these on-going wars is that between the government in Muslim Northern Sudan and largely Christian Southern Sudan. The reason for this conflict is the insistence of the government that Muslim law, the Sharia, should apply in the South. Behind this insistence, however, is the belief of Sudanese fundamentalists that they have a mission to convert the whole of Africa and that the Southern Sudan is the gateway to the rest of the continent. But of course these matters spill over into other continents. As I write, a hijack by Algerian fanatics has just been brought to a bloody end, which could have been much bloodier, in France.

I find it most distasteful to criticise the faith of so many people I admire and respect, particularly, the Sufis, who purvey a wonderfully beautiful and powerful expression of the perennial philosophy. However, to my mind the Muslim fundamentalists are no more true Muslims than the Christian fundamentalists are true Christians.

In saying this, I am bearing in mind another piece of bad news: that the majority party in both the US Senate and House of Representatives contains a significant proportion of fanatical Christians. These, however, are not the self-sacrificing poor who mostly become the Muslim extremists, but the comfortable fat cats whose enemies are not so much oppressors and/or heretics, but any whom they feel to threaten their cosy creed and privileged way of life — immigrants, the poor, political mavericks, women who want control over their own bodies. They find it easy enough to distort scripture to justify their hates. It is not too fanciful to imagine a renewal of McCarthyism, or even some sort of 'holy war' (probably fought by proxy) with an Islamic enemy.

The hesitation, bickering and inconclusive arguing over Bosnia have, if anything, increased. The arguments go on interminably in NATO, the EU, the UN, and between a number of governments, notably of the US, Britain, Russia and France. It seems much more than likely that the Bosnian Serbs will get what they want. But even if there is a settlement within the formal frontiers of Bosnia, many issues will remain unresolved. What about the large areas of Croatia now occupied by Serbs and called the Serb Republic of Krajina? Osijek, it must be remembered, is enclosed on three sides by this gawky self-styled republic: will the Croatians try to recapture this territory? Will the Serbs renew their efforts to overrun Osijek?

But quite apart from the problems of Bosnia itself, what does indecision over that unhappy land bode for the rest of Europe? Will conflict(s) in the Caucasus affect it? How will European policy respond in future to the probably continuing and quite likely increasing flow of refugees and immigrants? Is it possible to identify any indications that the useless violence and insensate cruelty that impelled me to write this book is on the wane? When the leader of one of the worlds' great nations is responsible, in the name of democracy, for a huge atrocity where can we find encouragement? When every news bulletin and daily paper reports more brutality inflicted on, and not infrequently by, children, how can we have faith in progress?

Reviewing the flow of news has merely strengthened my conviction that a great deal in our interpersonal, social and international relations has gone wrong to the extent and with the effect that existing remedies are of little use. The police can't cope with juvenile crime any more than the UN can cope with wars of infantile folly. The institutions of the human race as a whole have lost whatever capacity they may have had to deal with the pointless violence of desperation and alienation.

But we, as individuals, are able to. We are able to heal ourselves and to spread the healing around us and into our own community so that healed communities come into being.

This is the lesson taught by countless good women and men, and by the Osijeks of the world. It is a lesson we can learn and teach every day. We can learn it because we all, in some degree, suffer from the same soul wound. We can teach because of the unlimited potential we all share for wisdom, courage and compassion. We need it, because of our lack of awareness; we can give it, because since we all have some measure of awareness, the very essence of Being is manifested through us. We need it, because we have become robotic slaves to a false identity; we can pass it on because our true identity, even if concealed by ego, is always with us.

Indeed, we cannot help passing it on, because the recognition of the reality of ourselves is inseparable from the recognition of the reality of others; and this inevitably moves them.

This transformation through shared humanity may seem a slow, weak tool, perilously depending on the vulnerable individual. True. It would be pleasant to be able to believe that some mass imposition of, say, communism or some other political or religious ideology could change us into new human beings. But the great faiths, as expressed through churches, have conspicuously failed to do this and in fact have often brought more suffering than they alleviated.

However, love, courage and wisdom are not ideologies to be turned upside down and changed into their opposites. They are not mental bacteria which corrupt the essence of the mind. The only quality they have in common is that both are infectious.

It is true that the Osijeks of the world are as yet few and far between, but happily there are literally countless potential ones. They can be found and helped to grow with a gentle, non-intrusive impetus from helpers who have themselves gone through something like the same process.

We must not forget, however, that those who are conscious of shared humanity may acquire, or even already be in some position of, local or national leadership. They may be able to shape events in such a way that wise policies affecting both human beings and environment are framed and implemented. Through such policies the people as a whole may be educated to be more conscious than are most of us of the needs and pains — and great potentialities — of others.

The Scandinavian countries come to mind as an example. Their policies towards the poor countries are governed by altruism rather than by self-interest (except in the very general and indirect sense that the alleviation of misery anywhere is of benefit everywhere); the government of one has actually given substantial aid to Osijek.

This is not to say that Scandinavians as a whole are more advanced spiritually (if that is the right word) than the rest of us. But their more enlightened consciousness would give them a better start on the quest.

Note on writing this book

Let me say that if I were completely pessimistic, I would not have burdened my old bones by the constant travelling I have carried out to Osijek and other places. Nor would I have taxed my mind by writing this book.

If we consider ourselves separate from what we do, we distort our understanding, both of what we do and what we are. The physicists, those enlightened people (though they do not always push their insights far enough), know that the observer is a part of the scene that they observe, and so contributes to shaping it. Not so the social scientists, certainly not the anthropologists (I mean particularly the ones who study what used to be called 'primitive society'). With the exception of a few, such as Colin Turnbull, they write as though their intrusions into wigwam, kraal, yurt, kota or igloo are unnoticed; that they are the proverbial flies-on-the-wall, watching the natives behaving as if there were no alien presence among them. In fact, of course the subjects of their studies had enormous fun at their expense. The anthropologists were studied as much as they studied.

I would find it distasteful and dishonest, let alone inaccurate, to pretend that I was not personally involved in, and therefore to some extent altered by, those situations I describe.

By studying situations we become a part of them, interacting constantly with the other actors. This cannot be dismissed as merely subjective, nor is it unscientific to draw tentative conclusions.

No, to recognise the reality is to be properly scientific. When we grasp the constant interplay of the observer and the observed we understand the inherent impermanence of things; all the actors, be they molecules or human beings, are constantly responding to all the other actors and to the totality they comprise. All are involved in the process of constant change, in the ever flowing river of existence.

There are, no doubt, some circumstances so well studied and of so general a type that, despite the inevitable flux, strong probabilities can be identified with some confidence. But not so in the circumstances I have been most concerned with: the complex relationships involved in giving and receiving aid, and in the efforts to limit or eliminate violence.

These are important points of intervention. The question is how people who are not an intrinsic part of the pattern of events, not members of the family, tribe, guerrilla movement or nation, should act; because in acting, they in fact become part of the pattern and so assume responsibilities for it. We know very little about these responsibilities and relationships, as a day spent at any conference on conflict resolution or peacemaking will quickly and depressingly confirm.

As a result of our failure either to understand these relationships or to recognise our implication in them, intervention often ceases to be constructive and is transformed into interference, sometimes with devastating results.

The antidote to botched aid-giving or peacemaking is what the Zen Master Thich Nhat Hanh calls *inter-being*. This implies a full awareness and appreciation of our interdependence with each other, of the links which connect us with our fellow creatures. These links are inescapable. If we are not conscious of them, we will be fettered and misled by ignorance; but the more acute our consciousness, the more effective our action, as I shall try to show.

These are the reasons for my decision to make full use of my own experience in writing about violence and the response to violence and to write about it in a way that does not disguise my personal involvement. All I can hope is that what I have to say may contribute to the store of information and opinion from which a useful if tentative set of conclusions can be drawn. Finally, I am a practitioner rather than an academic theorist. I am interested in finding the best way to do things and, particularly, to discover what are the best things to do in a variety of very different circumstances.

Postscript, July 1995

This is written just after my latest visit to Osijek and other parts of former Yugoslavia.

The recent military action in which the Croatian army recaptured, if that is the correct word, the Serb occupied area of Croatian territory in Western Slavonia, has obviously introduced a new uncertainty into the frozen violence of the Serb occupied areas of the country. Most people expect that the Croatian forces, until recently restrained by a now much weaker UN mandate, will take further initiatives. If so, how will Krajina react? If the Croatians try to retake the territories adjacent both to Osijek and Serbia, will the very powerful Serb army, the JNA, then intervene and renew its savage attack on the city?

My friends in the peace centre are facing the dangerously uncertain future with calmly purposeful efforts to expand their work. Since my last visit a number of developments have strengthened the trend for their activities to expand from the local to the wider national and international levels. This applies particularly to human rights, the provisions made for persons displaced by war and 'ethnic cleansing', liaison with the churches and ecumenical bodies, and to reconciliation both in areas where Serb and Croat populations are intermingled or contiguous, and through frequent meetings, Serbs visiting Croatia and vice versa, or coming together abroad. Possible future convulsions do not prevent them from planning, and indeed laying the foundations for, a strategy of reconciliation involving the cooperation of local and international agencies, official and non-governmental; this too involves much more than the Osijek area, applying especially to the more controversially disturbed zones of conflict.

I told my friends that the centre reminded me of a plant that grows in the garden of our home. It sends out tendrils which set down roots from which grow further plants which in turn send out yet more tendrils — and so on. The gardeners, however, authoritarians who want to preserve the bed for traditional flowers, call this a weed, invasive. They try to get rid of it, but it is tough and tenacious and has, moreover, a charming flower.

The groups of people working on education or human rights in other parts of Croatia are these new plants, their continuing connection and communication with the centre in Osijek being the tendrils. This seems to me to be a very sound form of democractic evolution. The centre does not become a dominant and centralising monster, but a source of helpful information; the new groups are not mere satellites, but separate though interdependent entities.

One such new entity is a peace group in the town of Zupanja. This is about two hours' drive from Osijek and is located on the river separating it from an area of Bosnia where Bosnian Croats are in conflict with Bosnian Serbs. The latter consider Zupanja as a hostile target and it has been bombed and then under shell fire for four years, ever since the start of this sorry cycle of current Balkan wars.

Two of us met some members of this small group in an infant school, where one of the members is the head. The more vulnerable side of the building is protected by tree trunks placed lengthwise against the walls. They provide some safety, but not from projectiles that land on the roof, as one did recently — luckily when the school empty. But the trees darken the rooms, which is particularly sad as the children are not allowed to play outside. Last week two children sneaked out to play in the open air. Their game was ended by a shell.

How can we bear such happenings? We have to turn from the path of history made by slaughtering infants, and choose another way. Even now, at the moment this page goes to the printer on August 9th, Osijek is coming under heavy shell fire…

Bibliography and sources

Most of what I have written is based on the experience of my friends and myself. For that reason it is impossible in most cases to illustrate or substantiate facts or opinions with the usual notes and references. But the great part of what I have to say is already well known to anyone who reads the papers and watches television. Probably none of us knows much more than very little of the wanton violence and cruelty, either in distant places or on our own doorstep, and what one of us is aware of is probably not the same as what a neighbour knows. But we all know enough to recognise the extent of our global sickness. So instead of trying to cite incident after incident, it is really only necessary to say: consult the media.

Of course, however, there are a number of books and other sources which usefully fill in details, supply figures or suggest ways of looking at things.

I will mention first a wonderful mine of information: Ruth Leger Sivard's *Military and Social Expenditures* (World Priorities Inc.). Most of the figures I quote are taken from the latest annual edition. Another very useful work is *A World Divided; Militarism and Development After the Cold War,* edited by Geoff Tansy, Kath Tansy and Paul Rogers (Earthscan Publications, London, 1994); the title aptly describes the contents. An interesting, but perhaps unbalanced polemic which highlights the aimlessness of violence is Hans Magnus Enzenberger's *Civil War* (Granta Books, London, 1994). *The True Cost of Conflict,* Safer World (Earthscan Publications, London, 1994) is a source of alarmingly relevant information.

Among countless volumes on European history, I have found Eric Hobsbawm's *Age of Extremes* (Michael Joseph, London, 1994) extremely useful for the present century, and Henry Kamer's *European Society: 1500-1700* (R, London, 1992) for another very significant period. A superb analysis of the contemporary situation in Britain is by Will Hutton, *The State We're In* (Jonathan Cape, London, 1995).

There is a considerable literature on recent events in what was Yugoslavia. Since there was some concentration on that part of Europe in preceding pages, some examples may be of interest.

Yugoslavia War, edited by. Tonci Kuzmanic and Arno Truger (Austrian Centre for Peace and Conflict Resolution Training, Schlaining, and Peace Institute, Lubliana, 1992) contains a good collection of the origins of background papers. Another useful set of essays, particularly on the origins of the war, is edited by Sonja Biserko for the Centre for Anti-War Action Belgrade Circle: *Yugoslavia: Collapse, War, Cries* (Belgrade, 1993). *The Fall of Yugoslavia* by Mischa Glenny (Penguin Books, Harmondsworth, 1992) offers a vivid account of how (and perhaps why) war started in the region, as does the World Council of Churches' *The Tragedy of Bosnia: Confronting World Disorder* (Geneva, 1992). Perhaps the best general account of the current situation and its origins is by Mark Thompson, *A Paper House: The Ending of Yugoslavia* (Vintage, London, 1992).

I am particularly interested, of course, in the aetiology of aimlessly cruel violence, but here the literature is scanty. The concept of the soul wound, to which I have referred, is outlined in a pamphlet by Thomas Yeomans, *Soul Wound and Psychotherapy* (The Concord Institute, Pamphlet Series No. 2, Concord, Mass., USA, 1994). Erich Fromm's *The Anatomy of Human Destructiveness* (London, 1977) is a comprehensive account of violence which provides a framework for the crucial questions; these are directly addressed by Felicity de Zulueta in *From Pain to Violence: The Traumatic Roots of Destructiveness* (W. Whurr, London, 1993). Her conclusions, based on a comprehensive study of the literature, appear to be congruent with mine. I also referred to the concept of the malign reptilian brain. This is very interestingly examined by Frank Cawson in *The Monsters in the Mind — The Face of Evil in Myth, Legend and Contemporary Life* (Book Guild, 1995).

In the field of development, Jeremy Seabrook's *Victim of Development: Resistance and Alternatives* (Verso, London and New York, 1993) is essential, illuminating and horrifying. So also is another quite different work, Dervla Murphy's account of a bicycle ride from Kenya to Zimbabwe, *The Ukinwi Road* (John Murray, London, 1993), during which she not only observed but experienced the results of failed development efforts by the IMF and other bodies as well as the devastating ravages of Ukinwi, the Swahili word for AIDS.

Issues of development, and of course of war, have enormous implications for the environment. Here, indispensible books are Ken Jones' *Beyond Optimism* (Jon Carpenter, Oxford, 1993) and also his *The Social Face of Buddhism* (Wisdom Books, London, 1989). The Buddhist slant of these two works informs my thinking on both social and related environmental questions.

This brings me to the sources influencing this book's general approach to its subject matter. For the first, I must go very far back to my boyhood, when R H Tawney's *Religion and the Rise of Capitalism* (Faber, London, 1923) made a lasting impression. Next came the orientation of the Tavistock Institute of Human Relations, combining eclectic social science with psychoanalysis. This is best represented collectively in *The Social Engagement of Social Science: A Tavistock Anthology; Volume 1: The Socio-Psychological Perspective*, edited by Eric Trist and Hugh Murray (The University of Pennsylvania Press, Philadelphia, 1990). This contains an article by myself and two others on the subject of prisoner of war resettlement referred to in this work.

The worlds of science and Eastern religion meet in Fritjof Capra's *The Turning Point: Science, Society and the Rising Culture* (Wildwood House, London, 1985), which applies the principle of interdependence to several of the social and physical sciences.

My understanding of social issues (or, perhaps better, the absolute interdependence of what we might consider separately as social and human affairs) derived in a very general way from the structural anthropology of Radcliffe Brown and Malinowski (though they would have strongly rejected the relevance of psychology). But more recently I have learned much from Buddhism, especially the Tibetan traditions, also from Thich Nhat Hahn, a Zen Master from Vietnam, in for example *The Heart of Understanding* (The Parallax Press, Berkeley, Ca., 1988). I have been privileged to learn from the Dalai Lama himself and his many writings, including *A Human Approach to World Peace* (Wisdom Publications, London, 1984) and *Universal Responsibility and the Good Heart* (Library of Tibetan Works and Archives, Dharamsala, India, 1984). The late Lama Thubten Yeshe's *Introduction to Tantra: A Vision of Totality* (Wisdom Publications, London, 1987) has been most significant for me, and Geshe Kelsang Gyatso's *Buddhism in the Tibetan Tradition: A Guide* (Routledge and Kegan Paul, London and New York, 1984) is a most helpful introduction to what is for many a completely new way of looking at the world.

Index